BULGARIA
AND THE BULGARIANS
A BRIEF HISTORY

PLAMEN PAVLOV

BULGARIA
AND THE BULGARIANS

A BRIEF HISTORY

BORINA

Second edition, 2013

First edition in Bulgaria, 2009
Borina Publishing House

E-mail: borina@borina.com
www.borina.com

CONTENTS

COAT-OF-ARMS OF THE REPUBLIC OF BULGARIA

The Coat of Arms of the Republic of Bulgaria depicts a crowned gold lion rampant on a dark gules shield. Above the shield there is a large crown the archetype of which is the crown of the rulers of the Second Bulgarian Empire, with five crosses and another cross on top of the crown. The shield is held by two crowned gold lions rampant, standing on two crossed oak branches with acorns. (The three lions represent the three parts of Bulgaria: Moesia, Thrace, and Macedonia.) Under the shield there is a white band, lined with the national colors, containing the text 'Saedinenieto pravi silata' ('Union Produces Strength').

NATIONAL FLAG OF THE REPUBLIC OF BULGARIA

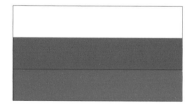

The Flag of the Republic of Bulgaria is a tricolor: white, green, and red bands arranged horizontally from top down.

BRIEF INFORMATION

Bulgaria is a republic in SouthEastern Europe. Situated in the Balkan Peninsula, Bulgaria borders in the north on Romania, in the east on the Black Sea, in the south on Turkey and Greece, and in the west on the Republic of Serbia and the Former Yugoslav Republic of Macedonia.

The surface area of Bulgaria is 110,993 km² (42,823 sq. miles). The greatest distance from north to south is about 330 km (about 210 miles) and from east to west, about 500 km (about 310 miles).

The population of Bulgaria according to the 2011 census is 7,364,570 people. About 85 percent of the population are ethnic Bulgarians and 9 percent are Turks. Small minorities of Armenians, Roma (Gypsies) and Greeks also live in the country.

Sofia is the capital and the biggest city of Bulgaria (1,291,591 inhabitants). Other major cities are Plovdiv (341,374) and Varna (308,601), the country's coastal capital and main seaport.

The official language is Bulgarian, spoken by about 90 percent of the population.

Religion: almost 80 percent of the population are Christian with 76% professing Orthodox Christianity. The second largest religious community is the Muslim – about 10%. There are also Jews, Catholic and Protestant Christians.

The state system is a parliamentary republic with unicameral parliament (National Assembly) consisting of 240 deputies with a 4-year mandate. Head of State is the President with a 5-year term of office. Central executive body is the Council of Ministers.

The monetary unit of the country is the Lev (international code BGN); 1 lev contains 100 stotinki. Notes are of denominations of 1, 2, 5, 10, 20, 50 and 100 lev, while coins are 1, 2, 5, 10, 20, 50 stotinki and 1 lev. Since 1999 the Lev has been pegged initially to the German mark and later to the euro: 1 EUR =1.956 BGN.

March 3 is the National Holiday.

Bulgaria is a fully-fledged member of the European Union since 1 January 2007.

DISCOVER BULGARIA!

In the land of the Bulgarians the inquiring eye will see, laid one upon the other, historical epochs and civilizations of indisputable importance to Europe and to the world. The extremely ancient and diverse cultural-historical heritage of Bulgaria is in chime with her beautiful nature and temperate, healthful climate. The country's cross-road geographical location has made it, from the hoary antiquity, a centre of busy contacts between peoples and civilizations from the Mediterranean, the Near- and the Middle East, Eastern and Middle Europe. Unfortunately, historical vicissitudes in the

Items of prehistoric plastic art. These illustrate the advent of the first anthropomorphic Gods and Goddesses to Europe and are actually models of dwellings, mountain (cave) and settlement sanctuaries for the population in 'The Land of Trake" (Thrace); 6ᵗʰ – 5ᵗʰ millennium BC.

National Park 'Pirin': The Nag
Bulgarian Black Sea Coast: Cape Chirakman
River Arda valley
Belogradchik Rocks: a candidate for one of the new set of
seven wonders of the world
The Biosphere Reserve 'Srebarna'

course of several centuries have left the ancient Bulgarian land in the 'periphery of Europe'. This holds true with particular force for the turbulent 20th century AD marked by the two slaughterous global conflicts, the Cold War that followed, and the confrontation between the two most powerful political blocs. The return of Bulgaria to the family of the European democracies by the end of the 20th century opened new opportunities for millions of people from Europe and from the whole world to carry into effect their own 'discovery of Bulgaria'.

'PRE-HISTORIC' AND 'ANCIENT' BULGARIA

FIRST MEN IN EUROPE

In the 19th – 20th centuries AD it was thought that the ancient 'pre-human' had passed from Africa to Europe crossing the Gibraltar Straits, Spain and Southern France. Other hypotheses were looking for this 'bridge' in Sicily and Italy. By the end of the 20th century French and Bulgarian archaeologists revealed the secrets of the cave named 'Kozarnika' near the Stara Planina town of Belogradchik. It was exactly there, in that

cave that the oldest traces from the presence of a pre-human being in Europe (1.4-1.6 millions of years ago) had been found out. Inside that cave archaeologists found a piece of bone covered with mysterious notches: the most ancient evidence of intelligent activity found so far anywhere in the world! The monuments of human activity during the Paleolithic Age had multiplied in time 'only' 200 000 years ago. Traces from the 'able man' (Homo habilis) have been found out near Nikopol, Devnya, in the Rodopi Mountains

The cave 'Kozarnika', near the railway station Oreshets, district of Belogradchik: during archaeological excavations carried out by a French-Bulgarian team, the earliest human presence in Europe was found out there, which was dated at 1.5 million of years ago. Archaeologists also found a bone with traces of 'symbolic thinking' from the same epoch.

Devetashka cave: one of the biggest and most important human dwellings in South-East Europe. The cave was inhabited both during the Middle (120 000 – 40 000 BC) and the Late (40 000 – 10 000 BC) Paleolithic Age, and during the Copper and Stone Age, the Bronze and the Iron Age and in the course of almost three centuries had also been a Thracian sanctuary.

The cave 'Magourata', district of Belogradchik: Late Paleolithic Age paintings dated 10 000 – 9000 BC. The cave sanctuary is located at 500 m from the cave entrance and pictures of different ages were found in it. They were painted with natural ochre and bats' guano; the oldest ones were dated from the Late Paleolithic Age.

and elsewhere, and from the Neanderthal Man who succeeded him some 120 000 years ago in the caves 'Bacho Kiro' (near Dryanovo monastery), 'Devetashka' (region of Lovesh), 'Samouilitsa-II' (near the village of Kounino, region of Vratsa), etc. That pre-human being had developed a real 'flint industry', had organized hunting of large animals (mammoths, cave bears, deer), improving and making the cave-dwellings more comfortable, etc. The rudiments of art, of religious concepts and rites had appeared, too. In Bulgarian lands scientists and researchers came across some extremely early manifestations of division and specialization of labour: a workshop for manufacturing flint spear gads as old as 45 000 years was found in a Paleolithic settlement near the village of Mousselievo (not far from the Danube town of Nikopol) by the river Osam. During the Late Paleolithic Age (40 000 – 10 000 BC) came the end of the last Ice Age (Glacial Period) and the contemporary, Cro-Magnon man (Homo sapiens), hascome into being. A revolution of its own in man's activities, in his social and spiritual life had taken place. The primitive human herd had irreversibly transformed itself into a society.

CRADLE OF EUROPEAN CIVILIZATION

The Neolithic (New Stone) Age (7000-5000 BC) was the key time for the overall development of humanity. The Neolithic Age first 'territory' in Europe was the Balkan Peninsula and its most powerful focus was Thrace. Research carried out at the settlement barrows revealed the existence of 'modern', 'producing' society in which the leading sector was agriculture. Ceramics emerged – an industry that has accompanied man's everyday life for thousand of years. Weaving came into existence, too and on some statuettes from that period one can see the clothes of that time. Two Neolithic settlements from the middle of the 4th millennium BC have been exhibited in Sta-

ra Zagora: they have the best preserved dead stock found so far in Europe. Hundreds of settlements have been studied in Bulgaria, some of them have become benchmarks for the European archaeology: at the village of Kapitan Dimitrievo (near Rodopi town of Peshtera), Galabnik (region of Pernik), Slatina (within the limits of Sofia), Dzhoulyunitsa (district of Veliko Tarnovo), Gradeshnitsa (not far from Vratsa), Ovcharovo (district of Targovishte), etc. At Ohoden (district of Vratsa) was found the well-preserved skeleton of the 'first European woman'. Even more ancient human skeleton was found at Dzhoulyunitsa, district of

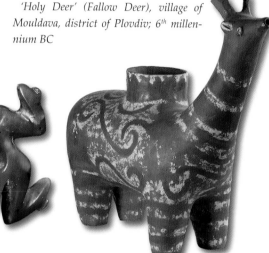

'Holy Deer' (Fallow Deer), village of Mouldava, district of Plovdiv; 6th millennium BC

Swastika-like amulet. Jade (nephrite). Kardzhali, 6th millennium BC.

Settlement barrow near the village of Kapitan Dimitrievo: findings from that barrow give an idea about the development of the Copper and Stone Age cultures in the Rodopi mountains and, in general, in the mountainous regions of Thrace during the 6th millennium BC.

Copper and Stone Age ceramics; second half of the 5th millennium BC.

Copper and Stone Age small cult tables and a model of dwelling; second half of the 5th millennium BC.

Copper and Stone Age portraits (probably of some gods); second half of the 5th millennium BC.

Veliko Tarnovo, from the time of 6100-6300 BC. The European continent had been irradiated by that 'Neolithic revolution' from the land of today's Bulgaria in the course of two thousand years.

The human progress was remarkable during the Copper and Stone (or the Chalcolithic) Age: it was here, in Bulgaria that the 'civilization of the oldest worked gold in the world' had been discovered, at the famous necropolis near Varna; here, in Bulgarian lands are the oldest copper ore mines (near today's Stara Zagora, Malko Tarnovo, Rezovo), a production facility for rock salt (near today's Provadia), sanctuaries, necropolises, idols, magnificent ceramic vessels… Some of these sites, for instance the settlement barrow at Karanovo (near the town of Nova Zagora), are a real, millennia-old book on the past of mankind.

Varna treasure with the 'oldest worked gold in the world' is of world renown. But even older than the oldest worked gold was discovered again in Bulgaria: the gold lamellae and the gold ring found at a pre-historic settlement near today's village of Hotnitsa (not far from the city of Veliko Tarnovo). The studies carried out at the Big Island in Dourankoulak Lake (by the village of the same name) revealed the largest pre-historic necropolis in

The first stone architecture in Europe: settlement barrow on the Big Island in Dourankoulak Lake. The two-storey building had been destroyed by an earthquake around 4400 BC

The 'golden' Copper and Stone Age necropolis near Varna: grave No. 43. The most ancient 'royal sceptres' were found in it (the grave of Tsar Dolonk, son of the nymph-ancestor Trake), while gold applications represent a stage in the evolution of Orphic traditions ('singing head') in Ancient Thrace; 4400-4200 BC

The oldest copper ore mine in Europe called 'Mechi kladenets' (Bear's Well), not far from the city of Stara Zagora; second half of the 5th millennium BC

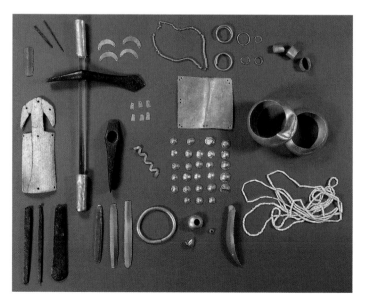

14

Amulet with the oldest pictograms (proto-script) in the world, from the village of Gradeshnitsa; end of the 5th millennium BC

Pintadera (a seal) from the village of Karanovo settlement barrow, district of Nova Zagora; end of the 6th millennium BC

Cult scene from the village of Ovcharovo, district of Targovishte. Illustrates the beliefs in the Great Goddess-Mother and the Three Great Goddesses of the three-seasonal animal breeding-agricultural cycle in Thrace; end of the 5th millennium BC.

the world (containing some 1200 graves) and the oldest stone architecture in Europe. A series of drawings found in the cave Magurata: images of men, women, various animals, a frieze of figurines, holds a unique place in the history of art in Europe of the Copper and Stone Age. Unfortunately the nascent civilization had fallen victim to dramatic events. These events have been explained with climatic changes that had taken place at that time and with the nomadic invasions from the north. Scores of settlements had been set on fire, the gravest blow having been the one delivered to the local population in the lands of today's North-East Bulgaria.

During the Bronze Age (3100–1200 BC) and the Early Iron Age the consequences of the catastrophe had gradually been over-

Gold decoration from barrow No. 3. An Early Bronze Age necropolis near the village of Dabene (district of Karlovo); second half of the 3rd millennium BC

A 'Trojan' type cup. Region of Haskovo; first half of the 3rd millennium BC

A dagger. Bronze. Village of Momkovo, district of Haskovo; 14th – 13th century BC

A Great Goddess. Ceramics. Necropolis near the village of Orsoya, district of Lom; 15th – 13th century BC

come. Thrace entered within the sweep of the so-called Mycenaean civilization. Social stratification was notable, a typical lineal aristocracy emerged with considerable wealth at his disposal, taking a liking to luxury and applied arts. A typical example of the level of cultural development in that remote age is the famous Valchitran treasure dated about 1300 BC and consisting of exquisite gold vessels (totaling in weight over 12 kg) possession of unknown tribal chief and priest. In the development of this early Thracian culture there are many common features as well as regional differences. Particularly intriguing is the 'rock

Thracian dolmen at the village of Hlyabovo, district of Kardzhali; 11th-10th century BC

The Valchitran treasure. Gold, electron, amber: thirteen vessels of total weight 12 425 g: a large cantharos-like vessel, a three-partition vessel, a big and three smaller cups each with a handle, two big and five small disks; 13th or 10th-9th century BC

Rock niches in an ancient-Thracian sacral rock complex near the village of Nanovitsa in Eastern Rodopi Mountains

culture' in the Eastern Rodopi Mountains, Sakar Mountain, along the Black Sea coast. The megalithic monuments that have remained almost intact till our days are still powerful evidence of the very ancient past of Bulgarian lands marked by cultural phenomena like the mysterious rock niches (their main range is the Eastern Rodopi Mountains), dolmens, cromlechs and other impressive monuments of the ancient Thracian culture.

THE ANCIENT THRACIANS

Thracians had evolved as an ethnos in the first half of the 3rd-2nd millennia BC and were the oldest historically proved inhabitants not only of Bulgarian lands but also of ancient Europe. Thracian tribes inhabited the lands from White (Aegean) Sea and Thessaly in the south to the Ohrid Lake in the west, the Carpathian Mountains in the north and the Lower Reaches of Dnepr in the east. According to the 'Father of History', Herodotus "Thracians is the most numerous people after the Indian one.

Royal breast plate (pectoral). Gold. Barrow 'Bashova Mogila' from Odrysae royal necropolis near the village of Douvanli, district of Plovdiv; end of the 5th century BC

Sepulchral barrow. Odrysae royal necropolis near the village of Douvanli, district of Plovdiv

In each separate region Thracians bear different names but the customs and traditions of the whole people are one and the same everywhere." In the 'Iliad' Homer tells the story of the participation of Thracian tsar Rez in the Trojan War (13th century BC) as an ally of Troy; at that time Thracian or kindred to Thracians tribes (for instance the Phrygians) founded their own kingdoms in Asia Minor.

In the 8th-7th centuries BC Thracian coastal lands from the Bay of Solun (Salonica) to the Danube Delta entered the sphere of the 'Great Hellenic Colonization'. At that time were founded Byzantion (later to become Constantinople/Istanbul), Apolonia (Sozopol), Anchialo (Pomorie), Mesambria (Nessebar), Odessos (Varna), Dionyssopolis (Balchik), Tomi (Kyustendzha in Northern Dobrudzha or today's Constanza in Rumania), etc. To a great extent they emerged in the stead of or in a symbiosis with the already existing Thracian settlements. Between the ancient Greeks and Thracian dominated peaceful relations and a spacious zone of cultural interactions had been created. In political and military aspect superiority belonged to the Thracian states, which were neighbours to the Greek colonies. Among them the kingdom of Odrysae was the most powerful.

The Odrysae inhabited the valleys of rivers Tundzha and Maritsa, the Rodopi Moun-

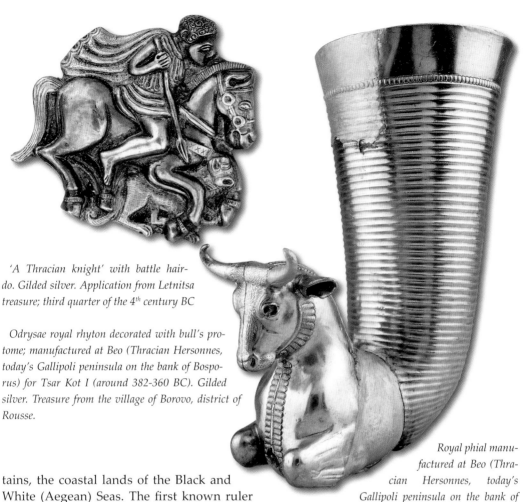

'A Thracian knight' with battle hair-do. Gilded silver. Application from Letnitsa treasure; third quarter of the 4th century BC

Odrysae royal rhyton decorated with bull's protome; manufactured at Beo (Thracian Hersonnes, today's Gallipoli peninsula on the bank of Bosporus) for Tsar Kot I (around 382-360 BC). Gilded silver. Treasure from the village of Borovo, district of Rousse.

Royal phial manufactured at Beo (Thracian Hersonnes, today's Gallipoli peninsula on the bank of Bosporus) for Odrysae Tsar Kot I (around 382-360 BC). Treasure from the village of Rogozen, district of Vratsa

tains, the coastal lands of the Black and White (Aegean) Seas. The first known ruler of their powerful kingdom was Ter I (480-464 BC) who ruled over the lands as far as the Danube populated by Getae and other smaller Thracian communities. Ter concluded a peace treaty, strengthened by a dynastic marriage, with the mighty Scythians from the Northern Black Sea coastal lands after which he directed his activities to the south-eastern parts of the Balkans. The power of the Thracian state was reinforced during the famous in those times Thracian Tsar Sitalk (444-424 BC). During the reign of Sevt (Seuthes) I (424-405 BC) the Odrysae' kingdom became the first-rate power in the Balkans collecting huge taxes from its subordinate Hellenic colonies on the coasts of the White (Aegean) and Black Seas. Interference of Odrysae

in the affairs of the Greek poleis reached its climax during the reign of the brave and unscrupulous tsar Kot I (383-359 BC) who infringed very seriously upon the interest of Athens. Impotent to defeat him in any other way the Athenian state chose to eliminate him by hired assassins... Kot intuitively made out the way of uniting the disunited

19

Coin minted by Alexander III The Great (336-323 BC)

Thracian royal coins

Thracian royal agreement under oath, in Ancient Greek language, by which the statute of the emporium Pistir had been stipulated. Village of Vetren, district of Pazardzhik; around the middle of the 4th century BC

ancient world but this was done not by Odrysae but by the ancient Macedonians.

Ancient Macedonians were a people closely related to Odrysae, Getae, Tribals and other Thracian communities. Their first known ruler was Perdika (around 640 BC). Among Macedonian tsars Alexander I, Perdika II, Archelai, Phillip II stood out. Ancient Macedonia had played an important role in the Peloponnesus wars and in the 4th century BC it became the most powerful state in the Balkans. Hellenization of Macedonians was more pronounced compared to the rest of Thracians but to the ancient Greeks they remained 'barbarians'. Phillip II (359-336 BC) subjugated the Odrysae' kingdom as well as a great part of the other little Thracian states in the Balkans. The world hegemony according to the concepts of that time and achieved by Alexander the Great (336-323 BC) attended to the interests of the then taking shape Hellenistic military-bureaucratic oligarchy. At the same time getting in touch with the old civilizations in the East influenced both the Macedonians and the other Thracian communities.

Along with Odrysae and Macedonians other Thracian communities also founded their own states. In the lands of today's North-Eastern Bulgaria and Rumania was the kingdom of Getae. To Herodotus they were "… the bravest and the most fair-minded of all Thracians…" The conquests of the ancient Macedonians took in only the lands of Getae to the Danube. The tribes that lived to the north of the river (known also under the later name of Dacians) continued the Getan state organization. They opposed successfully to Alexander the Great and his successors and later waged severe wars against Rome. They were subjugated only by Emperor Trajan in the beginning of the 2nd century AD. Another important state of Thracians were founded by the Tribals who inhabited the area from the Western Stara Planina Range to the Danube, between the rivers Iskar and Morava (the state territory of today's Serbia was part of it).

THE TREASURES OF THRACIAN CULTURE

Ancient Thracians created remarkable monuments of art and kept in close touch with the Hellenic and Asia Minor civilizations. The best known monuments of Thracian culture that came from the age of its heyday (4th through 3rd centuries BC) are the Panagyurishte treasure, the under-barrow vaults at Kazanlak, Starosel, Alexandrovo, Sboryanovo, the hundreds of sepulchral barrows (mounds), the rock cities and temples like the ones at Perperek and Tatoul.

From Thracian sacral pantheon via Ancient Hellas and Rome humanity inherited sacral symbols like gods Dionysus and Ares/Mars, portraits personifying music, culture and wisdom like Orpheus. The legendary Orpheus is a cumulative image of Thracian tsar and priest from Mycenaean epoch (13th century BC), re-created by his descendants in a 'heros': a man who had become immortal, who had turned into a deity. The leg-

Rogozen treasure. Silver: 108 phials, 54 pitchers, 2 cups, 1 skyphos (131 vessels are gilded) of total weight 19.91 kg. The royal tableware used to be manufactured in privileged communities among which one can read the names of Beo, Apri, Argiske/Ergiske, Geisty and Sayutaba

A Great Thracian Goddess. A greave from the barrow 'Mogilanskla Mogila', city of Vratsa; third quarter of the 4th century BC

Loukovit treasure. Silver: 15 vessels, 23 applications from sets of horse trappings, over 200 rings, semi-spherical buttons, tubules, small applications with portraits of Orpheus and animal heads; second and third quarters of the 4th century BC

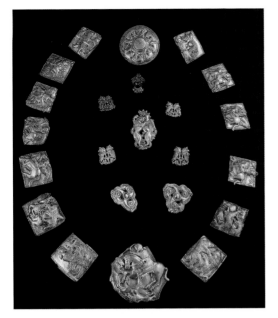

Letnitsa treasure: consists of applications for two sets of horse trappings; second and third quarters of the 4ᵗʰ century BC

Portrait of a Thracian 'knight' with an 'Orphic' head. An application for a horse trappings from Letnitsa treasure; second quarter of the 4ᵗʰ century BC

Detail from a vessel with a scene 'Trial of Paris/Alexander' depicted on it. Panagyurishte treasure; end of the 4ᵗʰ – beginning of the 3ʳᵈ century BC

Panagyurishte treasure. Nine ritual vessels made of 23-carat gold of total weight 6.165 kg; end of the 4ᵗʰ – beginning of the 3ʳᵈ century BC

Wall-paintings in the dome of the Kazanlak vault announced by UNESCO as a Monument of Culture; end of the 4th – beginning of the 3rd century BC

Wall-paintings in the dome of Alexandrovo vault, district of Haskovo; second half of the 4th century BC

The central funeral chamber in barrow 'Arsenalka'. 'The valley of Thracian tsars', district of Kazanlak; middle of the 4th century BC

A two-leaves door leading to the funeral chamber in the barrow 'Helvetia'. 'The valley of Thracian tsars' (district of Kazanlak); middle of the 4th century BC

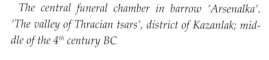

The ceiling of the Thracian vault 'Ostrousha'. 'The valley of Thracian tsars', district of Kazanlak; 4th century BC

A granite 'calendar' cassette from the ceiling of the Thracian vault 'Ostrousha'

end about the great Thracian conveyed by Roman poets Virgil and Ovid is well known by the entire cultured humanity. The Thracian bard has turned forever into a symbol of the creative genius of man himself. The characters of Orpheus and his beloved Eurydice had their own 'life' during the Middle Ages and in the New Time. Scholars have discov-

25

Ancient Thracian rock sanctuary and 'observatory' near the village of Tatoul, district of Kardzhali

A view from the ancient Thracian rock sacral complex 'Perperek' in the Eastern Rodopi mountains

A vault from the region of Sveshtari with sculptured caryatids and painted sacral scene. An ancient Thracian sacral complex in the countryside area 'Sboryanovo' near the village of Sveshtari, district of Razgrad; end of the 4th – beginning of the 3rd century BC

ered in these myths a religious system of initiates tending toward monotheism in harmony with the monotheism of the ancient Egypt and the biblical Moses. Orpheus symbolizes not only arts but also the healing, divination, administration. The ancient ancestors of today's Bulgarians gave to the world the brightest example of the striving for freedom and human dignity, Spartacus, an Odrysae' aristocrat, leader of the tribe of Maedi from the region of today's town of Sandansky. He headed the uprising of gladiators, slaves and impoverished Itals that shook the ancient Rome in 73-71 BC. According to the contemporary science Spartacus was not a leader of a spontaneous revolt but a reformer who endeavoured to reconstruct and humanize the then cruel Roman world.

UNDER THE RULE OF ROME AND BYZANTIUM

In the beginning of the 3rd century BC the bellicose Celts invaded the Balkans. They establish their own kingdom with a capital city the name of Tille in the area of the Eastern Stara Planina Range. By the 320s BC the Celts' dominion fell down as a result of a powerful uprising of the subjugated Thracians. The liberation was short-lived as it coincided with the beginning of the Roman conquests in the Balkans. The Roman policies involved Thracian rulers in fratricidal enmities. The Odry-

sae' kingdom which was an ally of Rome managed to keep certain autonomy for quite a time. Thracians rose many times in rebellion among which stands out the one by the tribe of Besi led by the priest Vologes (AD 11). After the death of Remetalk III, the last tsar of the Odrysae, tributary to Rome in AD 45-46 Emperor Claudius transformed Thrace into a Roman province. Romans introduced and established their own social and political model manifesting a well-considered forbearance. A process of urbanization started and the following cities were turned into centres of the Roman civilization in the Balkans: Phillippopolis (Plovdiv), Augusta Trajana (Stara Zago-

Roman road crossing Trojan Balkan Range, which led from Ulpia Eskus, near today's village of Gigen, district of Pleven, to Philippopolis, today's Plovdiv
Roman bridge over river Borovitsa in the Rodopi mountains

28

'The Odeon' (the Little Theatre) in Nicopolis ad Istrum, district of Veliko Tarnovo

Ruins from the city of Ulpia Eskus near the village of Gigen, district of Pleven

The Roman theatre in the city of Phillipopolis, today's Plovdiv

The Roman stadium in the city of Beroe (Vereya), today's Stara Zagora

ra), Serdika (Sofia), Ratiaria (today's village of Archar, not far from Vidin on the Danube), Eskus (Gigen, region of Pleven), Nove (Svishtov), Durostorum (Silistra), Nicopolis ad Istrum (near Veliko Tarnovo), Martianopol (Devnya), Odessos (Varna), etc. During the reign of the dynasties of Antonins (AD 96-192) and the Severs (AD 193-235) Thrace, Macedonia, Lower and upper Moesia were among the blossoming Roman provinces, which attracted settlers from the Near East as well as Roman veterans. The Roman authorities, the demographic and ethnic contacts imposed the Latin language (especially to the north of Stara Planina Range), which in turn led to a pro-

29

The Roman thermae in the city of Pautalia, today's Kyustendil, had been built up around one of the hottest mineral springs within the limits of Bulgaria

The thermae in the city of Odessos, today's Varna

Remains from the aqueduct of the city of Nicopolis ad Istrum

cess of Romanization of the population. In the lands to the south of Hemus (the older name of Stara Planina Range) and in the coastal lands around the Black and White (Aegean) Seas the Greek language was dominating. The language and the authentic culture of Thracians had preserved themselves mainly in mountainous areas and partially in Moesia.

From the mid-3rd century AD the Roman Empire started wars with the German people of Goths. In a battle against them near the city of Abritus (today's Razgrad) perished Emperor Decius (AD 251). In AD 270-272 Rome was forced to leave Dacia; the province was 'moved' to today's North-west Bulgaria. The global cri-

sis in the Roman Empire had its consequences in the Balkans too, while the reforms of Diocletian (AD 284-305) situated them in the eastern part of the state. In AD 330 Emperor Constantine I the Great (AD 304-337) moved the capital from the 'old' Rome to the Thracian-Greek city Byzantion (Constantinople/Istanbul) called later by Bulgarians Tsarigrad (the city of tsars or emperors). Goths migrated in several waves to the Balkans. Nove (Svishtov) became the capital city of the first 'barbarian' kingdom in Europe. In a battle against the Visigoths in AD 378 perished Emperor Valent (at Odrin, today's Edirne in Turkey). Despite the migration of the two main groups of Goths to

A mosaic from Martianopolis, to-day's Devnya, district of Varna

A high fortified wall had encircled from all sides the city of Diocle-tianopolis, today's town of Hissar, district of Plovdiv

The Roman column near the village of Lesicheri

Italy, South France and Spain, their tribesmen remained in Bulgarian lands: the community of Bishop Urfila (AD 311-383) around the city of Nicopolis ad Istrum. The Goths' 'Apostle', one of the notable spiritual leaders of his epoch created the Goths alphabet and translated into the Old-German the Gospel and some of the Old Testament texts.

After the division of the Roman Empire in AD 395 Bulgarian lands became part of the Eastern Roman Empire (Byzantium) and played significant role in her economic, political, and spiritual life. Constantine the Great (AD 304-337), the founder of the 'New Rome', Constantinople, the patron of the Christ's faith, was born in Naisus (Bulgarian Nish of later times, assigned to Serbia in AD 1878). In the period 5th through 7th century AD the Byzantine Empire was governed by 6 emperors of Thracian origin, among these Markian (AD 450-457), Leo I Bes (AD 457-474) and its most remarkable ruler, Justinian I the Great (AD 527-565). Born in Durostorum (today's Silistra) is the 'last Roman', the great military leader and statesman Aecius, the man who defeated Atilla. In his turn Belisarius, the most remarkable military leader of the 6th century AD was born in Germanicia (today's Sapareva Banya).

ANCIENT CHRISTIAN LAND

The population of Moesia, Thrace and Macedonia was among the earliest followers of Christianity in Europe. The first seeds of the faith had been sowed by Apostle Paul himself during his trips along the White (Aegean) Sea coast when in AD 65 he reached the city of Nicopolis ad Nestum (near the village of Garmen, not far from today's town of Gotse Delchev). The tradition associates the Black Sea coast with the missionary activity of Apostle Andrew the First Called, brother of St Apostle Peter. Disciples of the Apostles found-

The 'Red Church' near the town of Peroushtitsa, 6th century AD

The 'Elena basilica' near the town of Pirdop, 6th century AD

The early-Christian basilica near the town of Belovo, district of Pazardzhik, 6th century AD

ed Christian communities in Phillipopolis/Plovdiv (St Ermus), Veroya/Stara Zagora (St Carpus), Odessos/Varna (St Amplius). In the time of persecutions of Christians scores of martyrs lost their lives: in Durostorum/Silistra, Tomi/Constanza, Tiveriupol/Stroumitsa, Phillippopolis/Plovdiv, etc. After the Edict of Milan came into force (AD 313) when Christianity became equal in rights with the other religions in the Empire, an ecclesiastic organization was built in Moesia, Thrace, and Macedonia. St Nikita Remesiani (AD 366-414) who was of Thracian origin, Christianized Getae, Scythians and the 'wild and fierce tribe of Besi'. He translated the Bible into the language of Thracians

The rotunda 'St Georgi' in the city of Sofia, end of the 4th century AD

The wall-painting decoration in the dome of the rotunda 'St Georgi' in the city of Sofia, 10th-14th century AD

Wall paintings in an early-Christian vault in the Danube riverside city of Durostorum, today's town of Silistra

The basilica 'St Sofia' in the city of Sofia, 5th century AD

(the so-called 'Biblia Bessica'). Local bishops took part in the dramatic ecumenical councils that took place in the 4th-5th centuries AD; and the council held in Serdica (today's Sofia) left lasting traces in the religious life of the entire Christian world.

33

BULGARIA DURING THE MIDDLE AGES

ANCIENT BULGARIANS AND SLAVS

The founders of Bulgarian state, the ancient Bulgarians (the so-called 'proto-Bulgarians'), were basically an Indo-European people, related ethnically and culturally to Sarmatians and other ancient inhabitants of Eurasia. Altaian, Ugro-Finn and other ethnic components were also involved in forming their community. The land of origin of Bulgarians has been looked for in Central Asia and their advent on the East-European political scene has been referred to the 1st-2nd centuries AD. Bulgarians had a diversified economy: nomadic animal breeding, agriculture, metallurgy, a number of crafts, building traditions. In cultural respect they have been under the influence of ancient Persia. A serious achievement is the ancient Bulgarian calendar.

In the whirlpool of the 'great migration of peoples' part of Bulgarian tribes had been carried away by the Huns. After the death of Attila (AD 453) and the disintegration of his 'empire', Bulgarians played more and more distinct role as allies or adversaries of Byzantium. Unrests and rioting instigated by the Empire weakened Bulgarian tribes which fell under the yoke of Abars and the western Turkic tribes. In the beginning of the 7th century AD rose the star of khan Koubrat. Being still a youth, he had been sent to Constantinople where he adopted Christianity, was given education and became close friend to Emperor Heraclius (AD 610-641). In 632 Koubrat threw off his subordination from the Abar khanate and Byzantium conferred on him the Roman title of 'patrician'. The 'Old Great Bulgaria' Koubrat had founded encompassed within its sphere of influence Slavs, Alanians and other peoples. A brilliant illustration of the power of the state and the high authority of Koubrat himself is the treasure found at Malaya Pereshchepina (not far from the city of Polta-

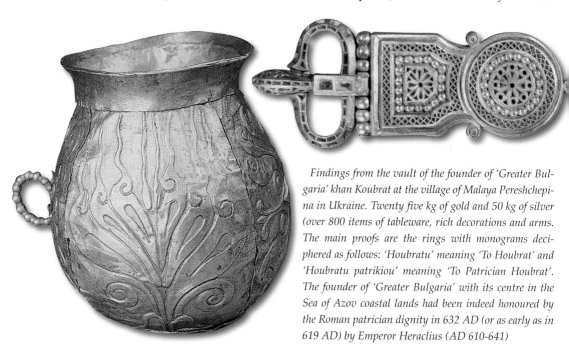

Findings from the vault of the founder of 'Greater Bulgaria' khan Koubrat at the village of Malaya Pereshchepina in Ukraine. Twenty five kg of gold and 50 kg of silver (over 800 items of tableware, rich decorations and arms. The main proofs are the rings with monograms deciphered as follows: 'Houbratu' meaning 'To Houbrat' and 'Houbratu patrikiou' meaning 'To Patrician Houbrat'. The founder of 'Greater Bulgaria' with its centre in the Sea of Azov coastal lands had been indeed honoured by the Roman patrician dignity in 632 AD (or as early as in 619 AD) by Emperor Heraclius (AD 610-641)

va, Ukraine), today exhibited in the Russian 'Hermitage' (Petersburg). This treasure contains Byzantine, Bulgarian and Persian precious vessels, decorations and other items (25 kg of gold and about 50 kg of silver) among which are the gold scepter and the gilded sword of the ruler.

In the 6th and mostly in the 7th century AD in Moesia, Thrace and Macedonia settled Slav tribes were called provisionally 'Bulgarian Slavs'. They had their own ethnic and cultural characteristics, language features, etc. distinguishing them from the neighbouring Serbs and Croatians. In their migratory movement Bulgarian Slavs reached Thessaly, Epirus and even Peloponnesus and Asia

A 'Map of Europe' after Muenster-Petri from AD 1626. On this map from his 'Cosmography' Sebastian Muenster shows the borders of 'Greater Bulgaria' (also known as 'First Bulgaria' or 'Bulgaria Prima'

Minor. Slav invasions became a constant phenomenon during the reign of Justinian I the Great (AD 527-565) and their having settled was most accelerated during the reign of Heraclius when the Empire waged a life-and-death struggle against Persia and the Arabs. Slavs had no experience in organizing and running a state; the coalitions between individual tribes were short-living; their princes were rather military leaders than monarchs.

THE FIRST BULGARIAN TSARDOM

By the time Koubrat died (by AD 650 or 653) the state had already been consolidated. In the later tradition a legendary story came into being about the precept Koubrat gave to his sons: he ordered his eldest son to break an arrow, which he did smiling and without effort. When, however, he had to break a whole bundle of arrows he found it was impossible… The wise Koubrat exhorted his sons to be united because in unity lies strength.

Old Great Bulgaria fell victim to the aggression of Khazars. Bat-Bayan, Koubrat's eldest son, was defeated and knuckled under the new conquerors. Today's Balkarians are distant descendants to Bat-Bayan's Bulgarians (residing nowadays in the Republic of Kabardino-Balkaria within the Russian federation). The people of Altsek reached Italy, and that of Kouber found shelter with Abars. The tribes led by the legendary Kotrag migrated to

The palace compound in the pre-Christian Bulgarian capital Pliska. Archaeological research carried out in the fortified palace centre of Pliska has revealed parts of the monumental ensembles of the Great Palace, the Little Palace and the Palace Basilica (the Grand Basilica); 9th-10th century AD

the north beyond river Don and later went to the middle course of the river Volga. There, between the 8th and 9th centuries AD was founded Bulgaria on Volga, the other great Bulgarian state in the Middle Ages. In the 10th century AD its ruler Almush adopted Islam. Until the time of the Tartar's hegemony in the 13th century AD Bulgaria on Volga was an important political and cultural force in the far north.

Of the most significant consequences was the migration toward the Lower Danube carried out by Asparuh, Koubrat's third son. Bulgarians of Asparuh settled down and fortified themselves in the so-called Ongle: the lands between the Danube Delta, and rivers Prut and Dnepr (in today's Rumania, Moldova and

Ukraine). After a decisive victory over the army of the Byzantine Emperor Constantine IV Pogonat in the summer of AD 680 Asparuh laid the foundations of today's Bulgaria, the oldest one of the contemporary European states. The ethno-genetic processes united into one nation Bulgarians, Slavs and the descendants of the ancient inhabitants of these lands (Thracians, Goths, etc.). During the reign of the Asparuh's successor, Tervel (AD 700-721), the state was consolidated, and Byzantium conferred on him the title of Caesar, the only such case in the history of medieval Europe! Among the most significant events in the history of Europe in the 8th century AD was the

A pitcher with the portrait of an warrior-victor from Bulgarian treasure found at the village of Nagy Saint Miklos (Hungary); 9th century AD

The stone column with the clauses of the 'Thirty-year peace treaty' concluded by khan Umortag (AD 814-831) with the Eastern Roman Empire inscribed on it

victory of Bulgarians over Arabs who had besieged Constantinople in AD 717-718. This victory was life-saving for Byzantium and cut short the strategy of Arab Caliphs for Islamic aggression towards the Balkans and the entire Christian world.

During the reign of the remarkable rulers Kroum (AD 803-814), Umortag (AD 815-831) and Presian I (AD 836-852) Bulgaria became one of the three Great Powers of the then Europe, dangerous rival and desired partner by Byzantium and by the Frankish Empire. Bulgaria expanded its territory far to the northwest at the expense of the falling apart Abar's khanate. In AD 809 Bulgarians captured the important fortress of Serdica (in Old-Bulgarian Sredets, today's Sofia) and going downstream river Strouma they made their way towards Macedonia and White (Aegean) Sea. The Byzantine counter-offensive in AD 811 ended in complete catastrophe and the perdition of Emperor Nicephorus I Genik. During the reign of Umortag Bulgarian frontiers

A miniature from the Manasseh Chronicle. Shows the feast held by khan Kroum (AD 803-814) after his victory in AD 811 over the army of Emperor Nicephorus I Genik

The medieval fortress Drustur (the Roman Durostorum) on the bank of the Danube: part of the fortified wall

reached river Tissa in the west and Dnepr in the east, and during the reign of Persian, to the Rodopi Mountains and today's Albania.

The first half of the 9th century AD was the time of state reforms and blossoming of the so-called Bulgarian pagan culture. As early as during the reign of Kroum a legislative reform was completed, while during the reign of Umortag the country was divided into 'inner region' and nine provinces ('comitates'). In the central power substantial role played the kavkhan (the 'second ruler', 'co-ruler'), the ichirgou-boila (the 'first minister'), and the coun-

Madara Horseman. This monumental bas-relief had been hewn at a height of 23 m into the living rock of the cliff at the village of Madara, district of Shoumen, most likely during the reign of Bulgarian khan Tervel who in AD 717 (and in his capacity of the Caesar of the Eastern Roman Empire) defeated the Arab army besieging Constantinople. A monument under the aegis of UNESCO

cil of the 'great boilas' (it should be noted here that 'boila'=boyar). The capital of Pliska was transformed from a bivouac into a monumental city with palaces, pagan temples, public buildings, bathhouses. Construction of stone fortresses ('auls') was carried out. The tradition of immortalizing events and persons of merits by making inscriptions on stone was given great extent. A series of gold medallions with the portrait of Umortag was minted, while the most remarkable work of the then Bulgarian art was the Madara Horse.

POLITICAL AND CULTURAL POWER IN MEDIEVAL EUROPE

The processes of the centralization of the state, and of the consolidation of its people, of the growth of the state international prestige reached their climax in the adoption of Christianity (AD 864), an act of colossal historical value, carried out by khan Boris-Michael (AD 852-889). However, the most conservative social strata rose in revolt against the new faith (AD 865) but Boris suppressed the mutiny. Political situation required that the Christianity be adopted from the old adversary Byzantium. Taking into account the actual position of Bulgaria on European political stage, Boris, with clever diplomacy, managed to win independence for Bulgarian Church (AD 870) but before he accomplished that, a mission of the papal Rome operated in the course of three years in Bulgaria.

In AD 855 the Byzantine intellectual of Bulgarian-Slav origin, Constantine-Cyril the Philosopher created the Slav alphabet (the so-called Glagolitic alphabet). Together with his brother Methodius he laid the foundations of the third classical language in medieval Europe, the Old-Bulgarian called frequently but inaccurately the Church-Slavonic language. Byzantium dispatched Cyril and Methodius at the head of a big religious-political mission to Greater Moravia. Cyril died in Rome (AD 869), and Methodius by Pope's verdict, became the Archbishop in the lands on both

Converting into Christianity of St Knyaz (Prince) Boris I Michael (AD 852-889) in AD 865. A miniature from Manasseh Chronicle, written by appointment of Tsar Ivan Alexander. Vatican Apostolic Library; AD 1344-1345

A page the text on which had been written in Glagolitic alphabet, from the Asemani Gospel. Vatican Apostolic Library; 10th century AD

The 'Round Church' in Preslav, the second (Christian) capital city of Bulgaria

The Eastern retaining wall (after conservation and restoration); end of the 9th century AD

sides of the Middle Danube. The German clergy dominating in this part of Europe opposed severely to the Slav sermon and after the death of Methodius (AD 885) the mission was chased away. The most eminent disciples of the Holy Brothers (Sts Kliment Ohridsky,

Painted ceramic iconostasis. Preslav, Preslav art school; 10th century AD. Depicted on icons are St John Chrysostom, St Ambrose Bishop of Milan (Mediolanensis), St Nicola, St Athanasius the Great, St Cyril of Alexandria…

Nahum, Angelarius, etc.) arrived to Bulgaria for which they '…craved for a long time…' returning to their natural ethno-cultural milieu. With the decisive support extended to them by Knyaz (Prince) Boris-Michael, the onetime monks' mission had transformed itself into the backbone of the rising Old-Bulgarian civilization.

In AD 889 Boris retired into a monastery of his own free will but his successor Vladimir-Rasate (AD 889-893) tried to take a new political course. At this threat to the new faith

Preslav treasure. The countryside area 'Katana' near the town of Preslav; first half of the 10th century AD. Among the treasure items the necklace and the diadem stand out. The necklace consists of 13 gold plates string together on a gold chainlet. On the plates and medallions the Holy Virgin, various saints and ornaments are depicted with enamel. The diadem also consists of gold plates. On the central one Alexander the Macedon is portrayed ascending to heaven on a chariot pulled by two griffons. On the rest of the plates show up the images of two dogs and various fantastic and mythical beasts.

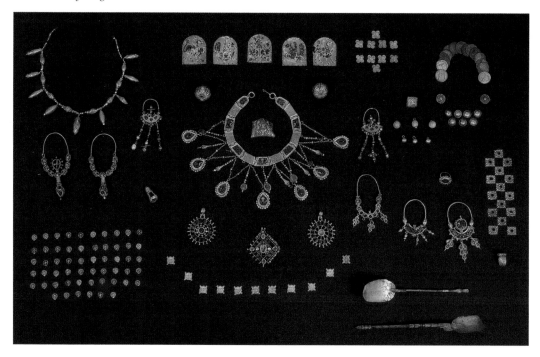

A miniature from Manasseh Chronicle. Vatican Library; AD 1344-1345. Shows a march of Tsar Simeon the Great in Thrace

Miniatures from the Chronicle of Skilitsa-Kedrin, Madrid transcript; middle of the 11th century AD. The lower miniature shows the battle at Bulgarofigon in which Tsar Simeon the Great defeated the Romaic army

Boris abandoned the monastery, deposed Vladimir from the throne and punished him by putting out both his eyes. The crown was passed to Simeon and the capital was moved from Pliska to Veliki Preslav. The final breaking off with the pagan past had been sanctioned by a 'people's council' (AD 893). After his death (May 2, 907) Boris was canonized by the church.

Bulgaria achieved the climax of its political and cultural power with the 'Golden Age' of Tsar Simeon the Great (AD 893-927). The third son of Boris, born as 'the son of peace' (AD 864) graduated the Magnaur School and was regarded as half-Greek (almost equal to the ancient 'Hellenes'). In AD 894-896 and especially after AD 913 Bulgaria took the upper hand in the military and political confrontation with Byzantium. Bulgarian hegemony in South-east Europe had reached its summit after the victory at river Aheloi (AD 917) and Simeon laid claim to the Byzantine crown. Bulgarian frontiers reached White (Aegean) and Blue (Adriatic) Seas and in AD 924 Serbia was transformed into Bulgarian province. The idea of 'Bulgarian-Byzantine Empire', of the rights of Bulgarians over the crown of the 'Christian Empire' was a key juncture in the medieval Bulgarian political ideology.

The greatest achievement of the tsar-'booklover' was the intensive cultural development. It had been not by accident that he was compared by his contemporaries with the great ruler from antiquity. Veliki Preslav became a beautiful city with palaces and a multitude of churches. The emblematic 'Round' (Gold' church', phenomena like the Preslav painted ceramics just point to the high level of the artistic tastes. The cultural elite included talented writers as Kliment Ohridsky, Nahum, Chernorizets Hra-

St Ioan Rilsky (John of Rila): the first Bulgarian monk-poustinik (hermit). A hagiographic icon from Rila Monastery (now in the National Museum of History in Sofia); 12th century AD

bar, Constantine Preslavsky, Ioan (John) the Exarch… Simeon's men of letters created the concepts of the new literary language, selected the most exact words, created new ones, etc. In his work Chernorizets Hrabar convincingly defended the alphabet and the language, a fact that made his writing popular also during the centuries to come. Preserving the Slav script was among contributions of historical importance Bulgaria made to European civilization. The Cyrillic alphabet was created in Bulgaria, a work of the men of letters based in Veliki Preslav. Because of its practicability it displaced the Glagolitic alphabet but borrowed from the latter some signs of letters as well as grammatical principles. Via Bulgaria the script and the Old-Bulgarian language had been adopted by other peoples too. Even today the Cyrillic alphabet is used in Macedonia, Russia, Ukraine, Belarus, Serbia, Montene-

gro, and for ages on end, in Rumania. In 20th century AD Bulgarian alphabet is used by 54 peoples in the former Soviet Union, Yugoslavia and even Mongolia.

During the reign of Tsar Petar (AD 927-969) a lasting peace treaty was signed with Byzantium; it was also strengthen by a dynastic marriage and brought as the most important results the official recognition of the title 'tsar' for the ruler and 'patriarch' for the head of Bulgarian Church. The country suffered from the invasions by Magyars (Hungarians), scourge of the then Europe, and Serbs managed to get free from Bulgarian domination. As a whole, however, Tsar Petar managed to preserve the role of Bulgaria as a Great Power as well as its extensive territory. The ruler took pains for the church, the favourite Bulgarian saint Ioan Rilsky was his contemporary. The 'Golden Age' traditions kept on further evolving in Veliki Preslav and in Ohrid.

A priest of the name Bogomil, a founder of 'heresy' persecuted both by the state and the church was active at that epoch. The Bogomil movement 'originated' in Plovdiv Thrace and was influenced by older heresies (for instance the Armenian-Byzantine Paulicianism) but possessed a number of original features. The Bogomil ideas, which regard the material, earthy world filled with injustice as a creation of Satan (in contrast to God's 'Heavenly Kingdom') had powerful impact on the Christian world in the Balkans and in Western Europe. The French Cathars, the Italian Patarene, etc. regard the Bogomils as their spiritual teachers and even regard themselves as 'bougres' i.e. Bulgarians by faith. These ideas, which the Roman Catholic Church persecuted severely and used to put to fire and sword, had their impact on the Reformation and the Protestant teachings in the West.

BULGARIAN EPOPEE

In AD 968 Byzantium threw the troops of the Kievan Knyaz (Prince) Svyatoslav on Bulgaria. At the tidings of the defeat of his army Tsar Petar had a stroke, retired to a monastery and soon died. His son, Boris II was forced to sign a pretended 'alliance' with the Russians against whom the Byzantine Emperor Ioan Tzimiskes had set off at the head of his army. He presented himself as an ally of the Christian Bulgarians against the pagan Russians and received support from a number of Bulgarian Boyars. Svyatoslav was de-

A miniature from Manasseh Chronicle. Vatican Library, AD 1344-1345. Shows capturing of Preslav by Emperor John (Ioan) Tzimiskes (AD 969-976) in AD 972

The medieval fortress 'Markovo kale' in the mountain pass called Trajan's Gates (after the name of Roman Emperor Trajan (AD 98-117). Via this mountain pass Celts, Goths, Huns, Abars, Magyars, Pechenegs and other invaders had forced their way into Thrace as did also the crusaders from the First (AD 1096), the Second (AD 1147) and the Third (AD 1183) Crusades

feated and forced to withdraw from Bulgaria. Then Tzimiskes threw off the mask, arrested the young tsar and dethroned him publicly in Constantinople. Eastern Bulgaria with its capital Veliki Preslav was occupied, but the western themata remained under control of Bulgarian nobility (Boyars). Boyars elected a collective proxy in the persons of brothers Comitopouloi, close relatives of the dynasty. They ruled on behalf of captured Boris and in AD 976 undertook a counter-offensive against Byzantine forces. During his escape to Bulgaria Boris perished and Bulgarians put up his brother Roman to be their tsar. The main figure however was Samuel, the youngest of Comitopouloi who, after the death of Roman, became Bulgarian tsar (AD 997-1014). Bulgarians won brilliant victories over Byzantium among which the battle in the mountain pass Trajan's Gate stands out. Anyway, the greatest economic and war potential of the empire had its say. After the routing of Samuel's troops and the mass depravation of soldiers of their sight (AD 1014) on orders of Emperor Basil II Bulgaroctone Bulgarian tsardom lost the duel that had lasted for scores of years. After the death of Tsar Ivan-Vladislav Bulgaria fell under Byzantine domination (AD 1018).

RESTORATION AND UPSURGE OF BULGARIAN TSARDOM

In the 11th-12th centuries AD Bulgarians rose in a number of revolts against the foreign domination (the most large-scale ones are those led by Petar Delyan in AD 1040-1041 and Georgi Voiteh in AD 1072); the country became field of invasions by the nomadic peoples of Pechenegs (Patzinaks), Ouzis and Kumans, Italian Normans and the passing of the first crusades. Many Bulgarians served in the Byzantine army and reached high state positions but the idea of a free Bulgarian tsardom remained alive. As a whole, Bulgarian lands were under the influence of the Byzantine economic and state model: so big landowning, money circulation, urban living – all of these were on the rise. Bulgarian aristocracy did not wish to accept the fact of its subordinate role in its own country, while those wielding power in Constantinople regarded Bulgaria as a conquered foreign area.

The crisis phenomena in Byzantium by the end of the 12th century AD intensified the anti-Byzantine trends. Brothers Theodore (Peter) and Asen, descendants of the Old-Bulgarian aristocracy headed the next in the row uprising. In the autumn of AD 1185, during the consecration of the church 'St Dimitar', the elder brother was declared tsar of Bulgaria. Defeated by Emperor Isaac II Angel Peter and Asen withdrew in the Northern Black Sea coastal area and entered into an alliance with the Kumans. Aided by the latter the brothers freed North Bulgaria and part of Thrace. In AD 1188 Byzantium was forced to conclude a peace treaty but their relations deteriorated because of the Third crusade (AD 1189-1190) and the alliance of Bulgarians with the German Emperor Frederick I Barbarossa. The Byzantine march to the new capital city of Tarnovo ended disastrously for Byzantines by an utter defeat (AD 1190). The energetic and rigorous Assen, co-ruler with Peter came to the foreground. Among Boyars started to brew discontent. The tsar was assassinated by his cousin Ivanko (AD 1196). Soon the usurper was chased away and Pe-

The church 'St Dimitar', Veliko Tarnovo; 12th century. This church was erected by the tsars Assen I (AD 1187-1196) and Petar (AD 1189-1197), the brothers that restored Bulgarian state organization

Miniatures from the Chronicle of Skiltsa-Kedrin, which show the blinding of Petar Delyan. Madrid transcription; the middle of the 11th century AD

The medieval Bulgarian fortress Lovech where a Bulgarian-Romaic peace treaty was signed in the spring of AD 1188.

Assen's fortress not far from the town of Assenovgrad, district of Plovdiv: the church-ossuary 'St Mother of God of Petrich'; 12th century AD.

An inscription in Assen's Fortress not far from today's town of Assenovgrad, district of Plovdiv, which runs as follows: "In the year 6379 [from the Creation], indict IV, Assen I, by will of God tsar of Bulgarians and Greeks as well as of the rest of the countries, appointed Sevast Alexy and thus this city was founded"; AD 1231.

ter again took the reins of the supreme power in his hands but also fell victim of a conspiracy (AD 1197).

The third brother, Kaloyan (AD 1197-1207), a bold military leader and skillful diplomat, ascended the throne. Bulgarian successes drew the attention of Pope Innocent III. In the autumn of AD 1204 the dialogue with Rome led to authoritative international recognition and concluding of a church-political alliance (union) but under the condition of preserving the orthodox dogmas. Good relations with Rome could not solve contradictions with the Latin Empire which emerged with the conquest of Byzantium by crusaders (AD 1204). On April 14, 1204 near Adrianopol (Odrin, today's Edirne in Turkey) Kaloyan utterly defeated the western knights till that moment considered invincible. Emperor Baldwin was taken prisoner of war and took to Tarnovo. The treachery of Byzantines led to punitive actions and repressions. Bulgarians accepted Kaloyan as an avenger of the evil deeds by Basil II Bulgaroctone. Bulgaria was transformed into the strongest power in the Balkans but at the time of the siege of Solun in the autumn of AD 1207 Kaloyan fell victim to a conspiracy.

After internecine war the throne was taken by Boril (AD 1207-1218), while Ivan-Assen, son of Assen sought refuge in Kievan Principality. The new tsar tried to follow Kaloyan's policy but suffered serious failures. In order to strengthen his authority, he convoked an 'orthodox council' against the Bogomils (AD 1211). In AD 1218 Ivan-Assen returned to Bulgaria and deposed Boril from the throne.

Second Bulgarian tsardom reached its climax during the reign of Ivan-Assen II (AD 1218-1241). In the battle at Klokotnitsa (March 9, 1230) he defeated the Solun (today's Salonika in Greece) Emperor Theodore Comnenus. The humane treatment by the tsar of the captured Byzantines and the support lent by Bulgarians from the White (Aegean) Sea coastal lands and Macedonia led to the expansion of the tsardom's land and Bulgaria already again bordered on three seas: Black, White (Aegean) and Blue (Adriatic). Devoted to the tradition that had been passed down the ages by Simeon the Great, Ivan Assen II signed as 'tsar and autocrat of all Bulgarians and Greeks'. After the relations with Rome and the Latins became strained and after becoming allies with the Nicaea Empire in AD

Tarnovo inscription of Tsar Ivan-Assen II in the church 'St Forty Martyrs'

The church 'St Forty Martyrs', city of Veliko Tarnovo

1235, the Orthodox Patriarchate was restored. A couple of ages later Bulgarian example had its impact on the church life of Serbians and Russians. Serbian Church became Patriarchate in AD 1346 with the support by the Tarnovo Patriarchate. Russia acquired its own Patriarch in Moscow in AD 1589 basing again its argument on Tarnovo example.

Tsar Ivan Assen II pursued balanced politics aimed at preserving favourable to Bulgaria status quo. The tsar kept a close watch on the situation in the East from where came disturbing tidings: in AD 1236 Eastern Europe had been overrun by the terrible Mongols (Tartars). After conquering Bulgaria at Volga, the Kumans, and the Russian principalities the dreadful invaders rushed into Central Europe. At the height of these events tsar Ivan Assen II died (around June 22, 1241).

The expression 'Ivan Assen's marriages' has become part of Bulgarian tradition: the essence is the system of dynastic marriages he used to implement. It also was representative of Bulgarian influence in neighbouring countries. The hegemony in the Balkans went along with economic and cultural upsurge. The capital Tarnovo turned out into a strongly fortified and beautiful city. Ivan Assen II erected the emblematic church St Forty Martyrs inside which, as a token of the ages-long state tradition, was installed the column with the famous Tarnovo inscription made on orders by khan Umortag with the wise contemplations of the great ruler from the distant 9th century AD:

'Man, even if he lives well,
            dies and another man is born.
May the one born later when
            looking at this inscription,
Remember the one that made it…'

49

POLITICAL CRISIS AND ATTEMPTS AT STABILIZING THE SITUATION

In AD 1242/1243 Bulgaria was overrun by Mongols (Tartars) and was forced to pay taxes to the 'Golden Horde' Mongols had established in the lands of today's Russia and Ukraine. During the reign of Ivan Assen's under-aged successors the leading position of the country in Balkan politics was lost, and in the middle of the 13th century the Nicaea Empire and Hungary occupied Bulgarian border areas. The power was partially stabilized by Constantine-Assen (AD 1257-1277) but Byzantium's alliance with the powerful Tartar khan Nogai (around AD 1274) contributed to worsening of internal situation in the

A wall-painting portrait of Tsar Constantine the Quiet Assen (AD 1256-1277) and Tsarina Irina. Boyana church in Sofia suburbs

country. In AD 1277 the uprising of the peasant leader Ivaylo broke out. He won victories over Tartars, routed the tsar's army and occupied the throne. Ivaylo was forced to fight on two fronts: against Tartars and against Byzantium. The Empire imposed on Bulgarian throne Ivan Assen III who soon fled from the country ignominiously ... Ivaylo was assassinated in Nogai's bivouac inside the fortress Isakcha (Northern Dobrudzha, today in Rumania) where he went to conduct negotiations with Nogai. In Tarnovo Georgi I Terter ascended the throne (AD 1280-1292) but he could not endure the Tartars' pressure. The throne was occupied by Smilets (AD 1292-1298), a Boyar from Sredna Gora Range who conducted a featureless politics of Tartar puppet.

In AD 1300 Nogai perished in a war against khan Toktu. His successor Chaka fled to Bulgaria. By his rigorous action Theodore Svetoslav rendered Chaka harmless. By skillful moves the new tsar strengthened his power, defeated the Byzantines and restored Bulgarian authority over the Southern Black Sea coast. In the winter of AD 1307/1308 Bulgarian wheat was the 'medicine against the famine' in Constantinople. Bulgaria gradually regained its positions in the international politics, and the Tartar hegemony was overcome. In AD 1323 the city of Vidin Despot Michael Shishman Assen became tsar of Bulgaria. That bellicose ruler strove to put up resistance to Serbian conquests in Macedonia. In the battle at Velbuzhd (today's Kyustendil) Serbians treacherously broke a concluded armistice; the tsar died some time after the ensuing battle from his wounds (AD 1330).

During the reign of Ivan Alexander (AD 1331-1371) the interference of Bulgaria in Byzantine internecine wars had as a result recapturing of Plovdiv and part of the Rodopi Mountains (AD 1345). With the powerful at this time Serbia good neighbourly relations had been established. Ivan Alexander's sister Elena, the most spirited 'first lady' in the

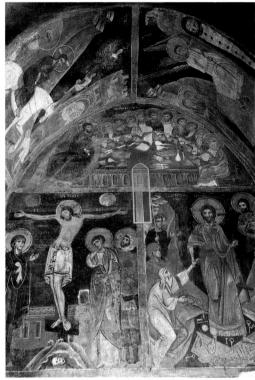

Boyana church, borough of Boyana, Sofia. There are preserved unique wall paintings from 13th – 14th century AD considered as the most valuable Bulgarian contributions to medieval European fine arts. A monument of culture under the aegis of UNESCO

Balkans in the 14th century AD, became wife of the Serbian tsar Stefan Doushan. The tsar sought to put under control the centrifugal trends typical for the 14th century in the Balkans by delegating the power in the most important regions of the country (Vidin, Preslav, Sredets/Sofia) to his sons. He was the first European ruler, who married a Jewish woman converted to Christianity, Theodora II (Sarah-Theodora). Unfortunately, the successor to the throne Michael Assen and his brother Ivan Assen perished in the struggle that had just begun against the Turkish invasions (around AD 1254). Ivan Alexander nominated as the heir to the crown Ivan Shishman, the son of the Jewess, while the senior Ivan Sratsimir, son of the former tsarina Theodora I was sent to Vidin. Bulgaria got involved in the events related to the advance of the Ottoman Turks into the Balkans.

The reign of Ivan Alexander marked a new upsurge in culture. The religious doctrine of Hesychasm which had started from Aton (the Christian Orthodox monks' republic) enjoyed his support. The founder of this teaching, St Gregory Sinait settled in Paroria (Strandzha mountain), while his disciples St Theodosius Tarnovsky and St Romil Vidinsky exerted strong impact on the overall religious life in the country. St. Patriarch Euthymius, disciple of Theodosius founded the Tarnovo literary school whose influence had gone beyond the limits of Bulgaria. The language-orthographic reform and

Ivan Alexander ('Tsar of Bulgarians and Greeks') with his family. A miniature from a Quadruple Gospel, written for Tsar Ivan Alexander (known as the 'London Gospel'), British Museum, London; AD 1356.

Wall paintings from the churches at Ivanovo rock monastery, the countryside area 'Pismata' near the village of Ivanovo, district of Rousse. The style, iconographic and art characteristics of these murals rank them among the best achievements of Bulgarian fine art from 13th-14th centuries AD. A monument of culture under the aegis of UNESCO

The rock sacral complex near the village of Voden, district of Yambol. It had started to function at least as early as perhaps the 3rd century AD and in the second quarter of the 4th century AD Grigory Sinait built up in this 'Border area' between Bulgarian Tsardom and the Romaic Empire the Hesychasts monastery 'St Mother of God', the so-called Paroria Monastery

the 'high style' of Euthymius were a model on literary life in Serbia, Wallachia, Moldova and Russian lands '… to the Northern Ocean'. The upsurge in literature and pictorial and plastic arts can be seen even from the scarce monuments spared by the fate: 'The London Gospel' (kept in the British Museum), Bulgarian translation of the 'Chronicle of Manasy', the murals in Ivanovo rock monastery and churches, etc. In the years of its wane medieval Bulgaria again had spread its spiritual influence over the Orthodox Slav world.

After the middle of the 14th century disunion reigns in the Balkans. By the end of the 14th century AD a contemporary wrote about 'three Bulgarias': Tarnovo and Vidin tsardoms and the Dobrudzha Despotate founded by brothers Balik and Dobrotitsa. In the mid-14th century in the Rodopi Mountains and the White (Aegean) Sea coastal Thrace emerged the little state of the famous Momchil, and after the disintegration of the Serbian tsardom in Macedonia emerged several small Bulgarian states. The strongest was the kingdom of Vulkashin and his son Marko ('Krali Marko' from the folksongs) with its capital in Prilep. Powerful ruler was also Constantine Dragash with a capital in Velbuzhd (today's Kyustendil).

THE OTTOMAN CONQUEST

The first waves of Turkic migration towards Byzantium began in the mid-11th century AD. As a consequence of the Mongol invasion led by Genghis Khan in 13th century AD, new Turkic tribes fled to Asia Minor. Their population expansion was made easier by the partitioning of the Balkans and also by the outbreak of plague in mid-14th century AD. The state founded by Osman and his successors became the leading among the Turkish begliks (principalities).

The first conquests of the Ottomans in Bulgaria were the regions of Plovdiv and Borui (today's Stara Zagora) in AD 1370-1371. Tsar Ivan Shishman (AD 1371-1395) was forced to conclude a disadvantageous peace treaty, strengthened additionally by the marriage between Sultan Murad I and the tsar's sister Kera-Tamara. In the battle at Chernomen the Ottomans defeated the armies of Despot Ivan Uglesh and King Vulkashin where also partic-

An inscription of Sevast Ognyan, the fortress 'Bozhenishky Urvich', district of Sofia: "I, Dragomir, wrote this. I, Sevast Ognyan, was 'Kefalia' during the reign of Tsar Shishman and a lot of harm I had endured. At that time the Turks waged a war. I sided with Tsar Shishman's faith." Third quarter of the 14th century AD

ipated Bulgarians from Macedonia (AD 1371). The Ottoman expansion became irreversible. Bulgarian resistance gave birth to legends and songs about Tsar Ivan Shishman, about the battles "... for the faith of Christ in Sofia plain". Sofia was captured by deceit (AD 1385), and after it Pirot and Nish fell in AD 1386.

In AD 1388 the Ottomans delivered new blow at Ivan Shishman in order to prevent him from a coalition with Serbia. Then followed the march of Murad I against the Serbians and the battle at Kosovo Pole (June 15, 1389). In the summer of AD 1393 Sultan Bayazid I surprisingly laid siege to Tarnovo and on July 17 the same year the exhausted capital fell into the hands of the conqueror. Residents of the city were put to repressions, 110 eminent Boyars were slaughtered, Patriarch Euthymius was exiled and part of the citizens, banished. Ivan Shishman kept part of his land with central town Nicopol and continued with his attempts to conclude an alliance with Hungary and Wallachia. On June 3, 1395 the last ruler in Tarnovo had been taken captive by deceit and decapitated. A year after that event the crusaders of King Sigismund reached Nikopol but suffered there a grave defeat (AD 1396). By the end of AD 1396 (or perhaps AD 1397) Bayazid took captive the tsar of Vidin Ivan Sratsimir. It seems likely that his son Constantine to have been left in Vidin as a vassal to the Turks. After Bayazid was routed by Tamerlane at Ankara (AD 1402) internecine wars broke out in the Ottoman state. Tsar Constantine (AD 1397-1422) joined the anti-Ottoman coalition instituted by Hungary together with his cousin Fruzhin (son of Ivan Shishman). The end of medieval Bulgaria is shrouded in obscurity but the fatal blow was the destruction of Tarnovo tsardom, the embodiment of the idea of Bulgarian state. The collapse of Bulgarian state, one of mainstays of the Christian orthodox civilization, was a grave blow to medieval Europe.

BULGARIA, THE MAINSTAY OF ORTHODOX EUROPE

Along with the Christianization of Bulgarian state in AD 864 the traditional for the Eastern Church cults of saints became part of the spiritual sphere. Bulgarian archbishopric instituted in AD 870, which had been raised to the highest rank, Patriarchate, since AD 972, enriched its spiritual practice with new, Bulgarian saints and cults. The Equal to Apostles Cyril and Methodius were canonized, their disciples Gorazd, Angelarius, Nahum, Kliment Ohridsky, Savva were canonized, too along with them, and their days are celebrated both individually and in a common day of the year called the Seven Saints; also canonized were the first Bulgarian archbishop Josef (Stefan), Knyaz (Prince) Boris-Michael, the founder of Rila Monastery monk Ioan Rilsky, Tsar Peter, Ioan Exarch and other honoured persons. In 11th-12th centuries AD Bulgarian pantheon was extended with the followers of St Ioan Rilsky: Prohor Pshinsky, Gavril Lesnovsky and Joachim Osogovsky, Michael Voin (11th century), Bishop Ilarion Maglensky (mid-12th century). The famous Archbishop Theophylact of Ohrid included in his works Kliment Ohrdisky, Enravota and Boris-Michael.

After the state was restored by Assens the 'Protected by God City of Tsars Tarnov' gradually acquired impressive sacral pantheon. The tsars Peter, Assen, Kaloyan and Ivan Assen II turned their throne city

into a "… second Tsarigrad (Constantinople/Istanbul) both in word and in deed". In the period from 13th through 15th centuries the relics of a number of Bulgarian and Byzantine saints were kept there: Ioan Rilsky, Gavril Lesnovsky, Ilarion Maglensky, Petka Tarnovska, Phylotea Yemnishka, Michael Voin, Ioan Polivotsky, and others as well as the canonized by the Bulgarian Church itself patriarchs Joachim I, Makarius and Joachim III, of the atrociously killed by the Ottomans 110 Tarnovo martyrs (AD 1394)

The most intensive cultural and religious contacts medieval Bulgaria maintained with the states and peoples of the orthodox community. Unvarying contacts with the Byzantine civilization as well as its own achievements made Bulgarian heritage property of

An icon of 'St Nahum of Preslav. Ohrid; the second half of 14th century AD

other peoples, too. The concept 'First-' and 'Second South-Slavonic influence', which actually is Bulgarian one, was introduced in Slavonic studies. The 'First influence' (9th – 11th centuries AD) in Kievan Russ was illustrated by the adoption of the Old-Bulgarian language, the transfer of Bulgarian books, as well as personalities as the first Metropolitan of Kiev, Bulgarian Michael (AD 988-992). Bulgarian influence affected medieval Serbia as early as the end of the 9th century AD. The second 'wave' of intensive Bulgarian influence was most powerful in the 14th till the middle of the 15th century AD. The presence of cultural figures of Bulgarian origin in Serbia, Russian lands, Danubian principalities was due to different reasons, included the role of Bulgarian monks in the life of the Monks Republic at Holy Mount (Mount Athos in today's Greece) and their closeness with the leaders of Hesychasm Gregorius Sinait and Gregorius Palama, and with

An icon of 'Seven Saints'. Ohrid; the second half of 14th century AD

Facing of the Souchava Quadruple Gospel; AD 1529

the then patriarchs in Constantinople among which was a Bulgarian, Josef II.

In 14th-15th centuries AD the names of the Russian Metropolitans and writers Cyprian and Gregorius Tsamblak stood out. Bulgarian influence was strong also in Wallachia and Moldova where Nicodemus Tismansky, Romil Vidinsky, Constantine Kostenechky and others had spent years in spiritual work there. Cyprian in Russia, Ephrem in Serbia, Nicodemus Tismansky in Wallachia are honoured as national saints in these countries; Gregorius Tsamblak possessed the unique quality of being representative of several national literatures: Bulgarian, Serbian, Moldavian, Russian, Lithuanian and Byzantine.

BULGARIA UNDER THE OTTOMAN DOMINATION

The fall of medieval Bulgaria discontinued its natural political, economic and cultural development; set it in isolation with regard to the scientific, technological and cultural achievements and inventions in Europe. The leading forces in a human society: aristocracy, intellectuals, nascent urban stratum like the 'burghers' in Western Europe, were destroyed or humiliated. Bulgarians were subdued to a bureaucratic and legislative system run by people and institutions of completely foreign, strange origin, religion, mentality. Discrimination showed even in some aspects of the everyday living: in clothes, church architecture (churches could not be higher than mosques), etc. The most monstrous was the 'blood tax': thousands of Bulgarian boys were taken away forcibly from their families and transformed into 'janissaries' (meaning 'new soldiers' or 'new army'), a cruel war machine constituting of people personally loyal to the Sultan and raised in the spirit of the militant Islam.

'Capturing of Constantinople'; AD 1453

Memorial complex in memory of Polish king Vladislav Varnenchik who led his crusaders against the Ottoman conquerors of the Balkans and perished in the battle at the outskirts of the city of Varna

Violence and discrimination had led to individual and large-scale conversion into Islam. The Muslim Bulgarians known under the byname of 'pomak, pomatsi(pl.)' live today in the Rodopi Mountains and White Sea (Aegean) Thrace (in today's Greece and Turkey included), in the region of Lovech, in Macedonia, Albania, Kosovo. Thousands of other Bulgarians lost not only their faith but also their language and identity. In Bulgarian folk tradition the synonym of conversion into Islam is 'turning Turk'.

Until mid-15th century the existence of Byzantium, Serbia and other states gave hope to Bulgarians that they would win back their freedom. In AD 1443-1444 they supported the crusade initiative of the Polish-Hungarian king Vladislav Jagelo (known to history also as Vladislav Varnenchik) and Janosh Huniadi. After the capture of Constantinople (AD 1453) the Ottoman State turned into a global empire of Islam whose borders in Europe reached Austria. As a main form of re-

A military camp of the Ottoman army (of 80 000 people capacity) near Sofia. An engraving by an anonymous (French?) artist. French National Library, Paris; AD 1788

sistance an original phenomenon came into being: the haidout movement. The haidouts organized themselves in detachments ('cheta'), which operated in spring, summer and autumn. Some of the haidout voyvodes were famous in their time: Chavdar, Strahil, Bayo, Karposh and many others.

The first serious failures of the Ottomans and the growing outrages led to the first Tarnovo uprising (AD 1598), which was prepared by the eminent Bulgarian Theodore Balina, the Tarnovo Metropolitan Dionysius Raly and the Dubrovnik trader Pavel Dzhordzhich. The help promised by the West never turned up and the uprising was crushed. By the end of the 17th century, when Turks were driven back at Vienna (AD 1683) followed a series of uprisings. In AD 1686 the Second Tarnovo Uprising broke out. Two years after it Bulgarians-Catholics from the Stara Planina town of Chiprovtsi rose on a rebellion carrying away with themselves the settlements around Vidin and Lom. After the expected outrages committed by Ottoman authorities thousand of Bulgarians emigrated to Wallachia and Hungary. In AD 1689 Bulgarians from Northern Macedonia, led by the Voyvode Karposh rose in revolt which in turn was drowned in blood. In 15th-16th through 17th century other local revolts broke out in Bulgarian lands; the Ottoman documents are abounding with information on haidout detachments. Irrespective of the fact that they were deprived of their civil and other rights, Bulgarians, leaning upon their Christian faith, the family, the village commune or the urban trade guild (an association of artisans like the medieval artisans' corporations in Western Europe) preserved themselves as a people. They continued their strife for political freedom even during the centuries when the Ottoman Empire was at the zenith of its expansion and military power.

CULTURE AND SPIRITUALITY DURING THE 'DARK AGES'

The Ottoman conquest delivered grave blow to medieval Bulgarian culture. The leading intellectuals (Gregorius Tsamblak, Constantine Kostenechky and others emigrated. The liquidation of Tarnovo Patriarchate deprived the country of its high regular clergy, of theological school... Bulgarians fell into the dioceses of three churches: Thrace and Moesia became part of the Ecumenical Patriarchate; the greater part of Macedonia was under the authority of Ohrid Archbishopric; Northern Macedonia got under the Pech (Serbian) Patriarchate. In spite of this, the literary life continued. In Rila Monastery, which was restored by mid-15th century, in the monasteries around Sofia, Etropole and at other places new literary schools were founded. With the advent of the printed book came new ideas from Russia, Western Europe, from the Greek, Serbian, Croatian and other literatures.

Church-donors' portraits of Sofia Boyar Radivoy and his family in the presence of metropolitan Kalevit. A wall painting from Kremikovtsi Monastery 'St Georgi' not far from the city of Sofia; AD 1493

An underground church in the courtyard of the temple 'The Ascension' in the town of Vratsa

An important part of Bulgarian culture in 17th century had been contributed by Roman Catholic authors: men of solid education who endeavoured to transfer the achievements of European science and culture in their homeland. Bishop Phillip Stanislavov issued the first printed book in the New-Bulgarian language: the collection 'Abagar' (AD 1651). The Sofia Roman-Catholic Archbishop Petar Bogdan Bakshev (AD 1601-1674), a man highly educated in Rome carried out educational work in Chiprovtsi and Western Bulgaria. He was the au-

The church 'St Ioan Rilsky' (St John of Rila) in Chiprovtsi Monastery

The coat of arms of Bulgarian Roman Catholic Bishop Petar Parchevich; 17th century AD

The church 'The Holy Trinity' in Etropole Monastery

Bulgaria's coat of arms from the 'Stematography' by Christophore Zhefarovich

thor of the first attempt at writing a 'History of Bulgaria' (AD 1667), poetry works, travel notes, religious stories. Another eminent Bulgarian from that epoch was Archbishop Petar Parchevich (AD 1616-1674), a man of great erudition, doctor of law. For decades Parchevich had been developing a diplomatic strategy for a broad Christian coalition against the Turks in support of a Bulgarian uprising.

BULGARIAN NATIONAL REVIVAL

The retrograde state model and the Ottoman Empire lagging behind the European countries eroded its war power. The Enlightenment reached the Balkans; the national ideologies of Greeks, Serbians, Bulgarians arose. The first representatives of the young bourgeoisie and the intellectuals of the new type came into being.

In 18th and particularly in 19th century the new economic relations made their way into Bulgaria, although not without difficulties; a brisk trade was developing; the first industrial and manufacturing enterprises were founded. In 19th century British and French capital also entered the Ottoman Empire, economic and other reforms were started. In AD 1834, in the town of Sliven, the first textile factory in Bulgaria was started, a work of Dobri Zhelyazkov Fabrikadzhiyata. Associations, companies, banks sprang up, too; railway and telegraph communications were put into operation. Also, in 19th century emerged urban centres with scores of thousands of residents

The bridge over river Yantra near the town of Byala, district of Rousse. Its length is 276 m, the width of the roadway is 9 m; there are 14 vaults with anti-icing (ice-cutting) structures. Master builder Kolyo Ficheto (Nikola Fichev); AD 1867

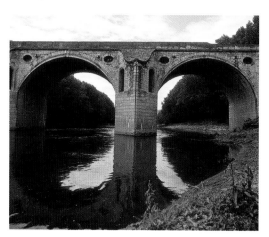

like Plovdiv, Rousse, Tarnovo, Veles, Bitola. Quite numerous became the medium-sized towns (from 5 to 15 thousand residents) like Gabrovo, Sofia, Sliven, Karlovo, Ohrid, Prilep, Syar, Tulcea, etc. Their aspect was changing; buildings were erected whose appearance was influenced by European architectural examples. Small (and not so) family-run shops (dyukyans): groceries, greengrocers', butchers' but also clothes, shoes, etc., inns, clock towers (as a symbol of the new pace of life) multiplied. In spite of the positive changes Bulgaria under Turkish domination continued to be an underdeveloped agricultural

The Clock Tower (1764) about which the Danish engineer Karsten Nibour who had visited Razgrad in 1767 wrote: "On June 22, by 5.30 pm I arrived in Razgrad. As I have not seen in Egypt, Arabia, India and all over Turkey from the Bosporus to the Balkan any clock on a tower, at last here in Razgrad I found one"

Zahary Zograf: a self-portrait and portraits of the abbot and the deputy-abbot. Wall paintings from Bachkovo Monastery; AD 1840

country with poor infrastructure, insecurity of property and investments, lack of worked and exploited energy resources.

The first national programme of Bulgarians had been worked out in the book 'History of Sloveno-Bulgarians' (AD 1762) written by the monk Paicy Hilendarsky. Paicy had become spokesman of the already aroused public energy; he defended the honour of Bulgarians and outlined priorities of the national development, reminded the past grandeur and angrily condemned those that had yielded to foreign, most often Greek, assimilation. In his book silently but insistently is presented the idea of the church's and political independence. Paicy laid the beginnings of the new Bulgarian literature and political thinking. His 'History' had been copied out in towns and villages and became a sacred thing to Bulgarians.

The most ardent follower of Paicy was Bishop Sofrony Vrachansky (AD 1739-1813). In his stirring autobiography he depicts the atrocities and outrages perpetrated by the Turkish authorities and the high Greek clergy. In AD 1803 Sofrony immigrated to Wallachia becoming there the spiritual leader of Bulgarians inspired with hope by the Russian-Turkish war (AD 1806-1812). As early as in AD 1804 two Bulgarian notables delivered to Sankt Petersburg a message from Sofrony. He raised the question of setting up a Bulgarian region to the north of the Danube and of liberating Bulgarian lands in the near future.

STRUGGLE FOR EDUCATION, CULTURE AND NATIONAL RIGHTS

Changes in Bulgarian society transformed education and culture into a cult: a phenomenon that astounded European observers. The ambition to quickly make up for the long ages of lagging behind the times was a powerful stimulus for prospering in personal and national aspect. The updating of education began with the so-called 'Hellenic-Bulgarian schools' the first such school having been opened in AD 1815 in the Danube town of Svishtov. Common urban schools where the standards of the secular education were finally established came next. Considerable role was played by the so-called 'Riben bukvar' by Dr. Petar Beron (AD 1824): an original 'bible of Bulgarian education'. A decisive step forward was made with the introduction of the so-called Lancastrian monitorial system of education: the first of this type had been opened in Gabrovo on January 2, 1835 with the handsome donations from Vasil Aprilov and the emigration in Odessa and Bucharest. Still more systematic education was given by the 'class schools" (in Plovdiv, Karlovo, Skopje, Rousse, Tarnovo, Shoumen, etc.); the students trained at them continued their education at high schools, colleges and universities in Russia, France, Austro-Hungary... Many Bulgarians became students in the Roman Catholic and Protestant schools set up in Istanbul (the renowned Robert College for instance) after Crimean War, in Plovdiv, Rousse, Bitola, Solun (Salonika), etc. Elite high schools were opened in Bolgrad (in today's Ukraine), Plovdiv, Gabrovo, a pedagogic school in Shtip (AD 1868), a commercial school in Svishtov (AD 1873), a theological school in Lyaskovets (near Tarnovo) and in Samokov. During 1870s Bulgarian intellectuals and financial circles of the emigrations discussed founding a Bulgarian university.

Typical Bulgarian phenomena were the 'community/people's cultural centres' (still existing today). School boards of trustees sprang up along with cultural associations and other forms of the nascent civil society. The more intensive contacts with leading European countries and Russia, the quicker growth of intellectuals had led to modernization of the cultural life. The New-Bulgarian (modern) language was being formed, in

Monastery school in the courtyard of the church in the village of Bozhentsi, district of Gabrovo

The fifth-grade school in the town of Karlovo

Aprilov secondary school in the town of Gabrovo; the first secondary school in Bulgaria; AD 1872

'Educational work', a bas-relief at the base of Vasil Aprilov's monument in front of the Aprilov's secondary school in the town of Gabrovo

The first Bulgarian school globe. It was made in 1836 by Neophyte Rilsky, a monk in Rila Monastery, man of letters, champion of the new-Bulgarian education; as a teacher he adapted the Bell-Lancaster method of teaching for Bulgarian schools

which the democratic principle prevailed. The new Bulgarian literature was being born, and the process of giving significance to the cultural and historical heritage had a high priority in the creative workers awareness. A typical example was the collection titled 'Bulgarian folk songs' by brothers Miladinovs from the town of Strouga (Macedonia). Poetry made its first steps in the person of Grigor Parlichev, Constantine Miladinov, Georgi Stoykov Rakovsky (the famous poem 'Woodland traveler')... Author's 'songs' by Dobri Chintoulov made exceptional impact on reading public. The first 'true' poet in the person of Petko Rachev Slaveykov showed himself. In 1870s universally recognized was Hristo Botev's genius, the first written works of Ivan Vazov were printed. Political journalism had its summits in the persons of Rakovsky, Karavelov and Botev, succeeded after the Liberation by Zahary Stoyanov. The patriotic-romantic stage-plays by Vasil Droumev and Dobri Voynikov (for instance 'Ivanko, the assassin of Asen') held special place in the public life and exerted unbelievable impact on Bulgarian audience in the country and among the emigration.

During the National Revival the architecture and fine arts had also developed. Grand master-builders like Pavel Iovanovich, Kolyo

Ficheto and others built churches, residential houses, schools, bridges. Towered the talent of Zahary Zograf, an artist who had created hundreds of icons, murals, easel painted portraits. The modern trends left their mark in creative works of Stasnislav Dospevsky, Georgi Danchov and Nikolay Pavlovich. Bulgarian science had also been conceived in that period of time and in AD 1869 in Braila (Rumania) Bulgarian Literary Society had been set up, which in AD 1911 developed into Bulgarian Academy of Sciences. Within a few decades only, in spite of the foreign political and spiritual domination, Bulgarian society gave rise to intellectuals with whom it entered the modern times.

Down the ages of Ottoman domination Bulgarians were deprived of their own church. Until 19th century the Constantinople Patriarchate did not conduct a national discrimination but the offensive of the Greek nationalism in 19th century changed the situation. The first attempt at winning Bulgarian own bishop was in AD 1824 in Vratsa. The 'double slavery' (political and spiritual) became unbearable. The reforms that were taking place in the empire after AD 1839, the consolidation of the bourgeoisie and intelligentsia further reinforced this Bulgarian activity. The mass movement began in Tarnovo, the biggest bishopric in Bulgarian lands and the protests spread in Rousse, Pleven, Svishtov, Stara Zagora, Chirpan, etc. The Patriarchate rejected the demand to have the chair given to Bulgarian enlightener Neophyte Bozvely. The leading centre became Bulgarian colony of many thousands in the Turkish capital city. Neophyte Bozvely and Ilarion Makariopolsky were authorized to represent Bulgarian community before the authorities (AD 1845). In AD 1849 Bulgarian Knyaz (Prince) Stefan Bogoridi arranged the first Bulgarian temple in Tsar-

A monument of the disestablishment of Bulgarian church from the Ecumenical (Phanariot) Patriarchate with its seat in the neighbourhood Fener in Istanbul. A lithography by Nikolay Pavlovich; AD 1872

A portrait of Dr. Stoyan Chomakov, one of the main figures in the struggle for Bulgarian independent church and acknowledging Bulgarians as a people of its own within the Ottoman Empire

A portrait of the first Bulgarian Exarch Antim I, elected by Bulgarian church people's council held in Tsarigrad (Istanbul) in AD 1871

Bulgarian 'Mona Lisa'. A portrait of Domnika Lamb-reva, sister of the artist Stanislav Dospevsky

A self-portrait of Stanislav Dospevsky

igrad, 'St Stefan' (AD 1849), the successor of which today is the so-called 'Iron church" in the city on the Bosphorus.

The Great Powers interfered in the argument on Bulgarian question. The attitude of Orthodox Russia, which sided entirely with the Patriarchate, was of special importance. In AD 1857 a kind of Bulgarian 'national assembly' was convened in the Turkish capital city consisting of delegates from a number of Bulgarian settlements, which again appealed to have Bulgarian bishops appointed. During the Easter solemn mass on April 3, 1860 held in the church 'St Stefan' bishop Ilarion Makariopolsky did not pronounce the name of the Patriarch and the multitude met with wild applause this act of breaking relations with the Patriarchate and this vivid demonstration entered the history books as 'Bulgarian Easter'.

The tidings about the Easter action met a powerful reverberation throughout Bulgar-

ian land and Greek bishops were subjected to boycott. Western states tried to use Russian obstinacy for their own advantage. The contacts of Bulgarian leaders with the Roman Catholic missions, the idea of union with Rome, the expansion of the Protestant propaganda, etc. led to Russians reassessing their policy. This was a merit of Graf (Earl) Ignatiev, ambassador of Russian Emperor to Turkish capital. On February 28, 1870 Turkish government issued a firman (decree) on setting up Bulgarian Exarchate. It encompassed 15 dioceses but did not cover all lands populated by Bulgarians. It was envisaged to hold a referendum (plebiscite) in Macedonia, which was actually held in AD 1874 and the results were clear: Ohrid and Skopje were given Bulgarian bishops. Exarch Antim I (AD 1815-1888) was elected head of Bulgarian church.

By setting up the Exarchate the natural boundaries of Bulgarian nation were more

Map labels (as visible):
Serb | Rumänen | Galatz | Tataren | Bulg. | Belgr. | Sarajo | Buk. | Donau | Schumla | Warna | Nowip | Nisch | Plewna | Osmanen | Sofia | Cetinje | Prisctina | Bulgaren | Phil. | Griechen | Elbassan | Bitolia | Skoplje | Osmanen | Konstant. | Skut. | Brind. | Gallip. | Bru. | Metzowo | Korfu | Janina | Lar. | Mytilini | Chios | Smyr. | Osmanen | Patras | Athen | Z. | Kreta | Griechen | Kythera | Rhodos

Legend:
Deutsche (D.)
Italiener
Rumänen (u. Aromunen [Ar.]
Serben (u. Kroaten.)
Bulgaren
Albanesen (Alb.)
Griechen
Magyaren
Osmanen u. Tataren
Farbige Streifung bedeutet Mischung der betreffenden Völker.

Maßstab 1:10 000 000   100 50 0   100   200   300   400 **Kilometer.**

Ethnographic map of the Balkans which reflects the German version of the ethnic situation in the Balkans following the Crimean War (AD 1853-1856)

or less outlined. The Sublime Porte was forced to abandon the ages-long used concept of 'rum-milliet' (*literally 'Romaic/Roman people' but interpreted by some as 'Greek Orthodox people'*) and to acknowledge the presence of Bulgarian nation. The spiritual unification gave birth to the first acknowledged national institution and in turn this fact raised, in the natural course of events, the question of restoring Bulgarian state within a comprehensible historical perspective.

"RISE UP, RISE UP, YOU YOUNG HERO OF THE BALKANS"

In 18th century the struggles for liberation had been linked with Austria and with the Orthodox Great Power, the Russian Empire. Bulgarian armed campaigns had taken place during the Austrian-Turkish wars of AD 1716-1718 and AD 1735-1739. By the end of the 18th century and the beginning of the 19th century the Ottoman Empire had lived through a period of anarchy, mostly related to the so-called 'kardjalii'(*meaning 'brigands of the plain'*). The separatism of ayans (governors of administrative provinces in the Empire) and the ero-

sion of the army gave rise to brigandage unseen until then by its scale. Some of the local rulers (particularly Osman Pazvantoglu in Vidin) even pursued their own foreign policy. Under these conditions the Ottoman authority allowed Christians to arm themselves and to erect fortifications.

Bulgarian participation in the Russian-Turkish wars from the end of the 18th and the beginning of the 19th century was on an even broader basis. On the largest scale it was in the wars of AD 1806-1812 and AD 1828-1829. An army formation called 'Bulgarian land troops' with Bulgarian commanding officers like for instance 'captain' Georgi Mamarchev, became part of the oper-

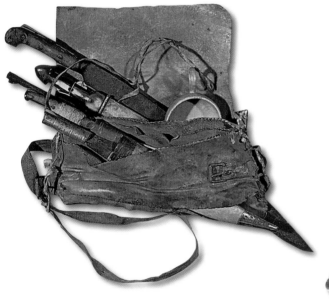

A leather belt for cold steel; from 18th-19th century AD

Cold steel (yataghans) and fire arms (flint-stock pistol and flint-stock musket). Haskovo Museum; 19th century AD

ating Russian army. Unfortunately the Russian-Turkish wars caused thousand of Bulgarians to emigrate to the Russian Empire, mostly to Bessarabia (the southern regions of today's Ukraine and Moldova) and Crimean peninsula. Thousands of Bulgarians also took part in the Serbian uprising AD 1804-1813, which actually was a Serbian-Bulgarian one. The nascent at that time Serbian chauvinism neglected the interest of its neighbours and went even that further as to seizing Bulgarian lands to the west of river Timok. Bulgarians participated on a large-scale too in the Greek liberation movement during which remarkable Bulgarian field commanders showed their qualities (the best known of these was Hadji Hristo). During the 'Greek conspiracy' in AD 1821 Turkish authorities subjected to repressions eminent Bulgarians in a number of towns.

A portrait of Captain Georgi Mamarchev (AD 1786-1846), an officer with the Russian army and one of the organizers of the failed revolt known as 'Velchova Zavera' (Velcho's Conspiracy) in AD 1835

The colours of the detachment led by Voyvode Fillip Totyu with Bulgarian coat of arms on it and an inscription which reads 'Freedom or death'

The next in the row Russian-Turkish war, especially the march of Gen. Dibich 'Zabalkansky' in AD 1828-1829, was accompanied by large-scale risings by Bulgarians. A plan was made-up of founding a Bulgarian principality, initially in Dobrudzha and a self-governing one like Serbia and Greece. This war again did not bring freedom, on the contrary, some hundred thousand Bulgarians set forth on the road of exile to Bessarabia, Moldova and Wallachia.

In AD 1835 Georgi Mamarchev and Velcho Atanassov organized a new, significant attempt at liberating Bulgaria: the so-called 'Velchova zavera (*conspiracy*)' in Tarnovo (AD 1835), which failed because of treachery. In AD 1835-1850 the north-western Bulgarian lands were shaken by a series of peasant uprisings. Atrocities perpetrated by Turks were particularly grave during the Nish Uprising. In 1850 the big Vidin uprising broke out but its spontaneity and almost lack of organization, lack of arms and the treacherous policy pursued by Serbia led to new pogroms. The riots in Braila in AD 1841-1843, which aimed at transference of large detachments into Bulgaria, had been frustrated by the local authorities in Wallachia. Crimean War (AD 1853-1856) brought again new hopes and tremendous disappointment to Bulgarians.

The beginning of the organized struggle for national liberation was laid by Georgi Rakovsky (AD 1821-1867), an intellectual, politician and national ideologist. After having acquired serious experience, Rakovsky set up in Belgrade, in AD 1862, the 'First Bulgarian Legion', which got its baptism of fire in the Serbian-Turkish conflict that burst out soon after. Although it did not transform itself into a liberation army (it had been planned to invade Bulgaria, reach Tarnovo and declare the liberation from Turks!), the Legion trained a large number of revolutionaries among which were Vasil Levsky, Stefan Karadzha and many others. After he got disappointed with Serbian policy and after fruitless contacts with Greece and so on, Rakovsky settled in Bucharest. He developed the so-called 'detachment tactics' for waging centralized partisan war against Turkish authority. Around the 'chief' voyvode a most radical 'party' of the emigrants had formed. Rakovsky rejected the blind binding in with Russia and was against the rising Balkan chauvinism. The 'Patriarch of revolution' could not develop further his ideas because he died in the prime of his life.

In1860s, in the emigration circles sprang up various political groupings. The conservative and pro-Russian 'Righteous Party' (the so-called 'Elders") was led by the wholesalers Hristo and Evlogy Georgievi. In AD 1866 Ivan Kasabov set up the Secret Central Bulgarian Committee best known by its programme of dualistic state (after the example of Austria-Hungary): the Sultan would also become 'Tsar of Bulgaria' and Bulgarians were to get broad autonomy with their own parliament, army, a Bulgarian assuming the post of high governor, etc. In AD 1869 similar plan was presented at Paris Peace Conference by the 'Righteous Party'.

In AD 1867 the detachments of voyvodes Panayot Hitov and Phillip Totyu crossed the Danube and entered Bulgaria. The magic word 'Comita' was born meaning rebel professing the formula 'Freedom or Death!' In Belgrade the Sec-

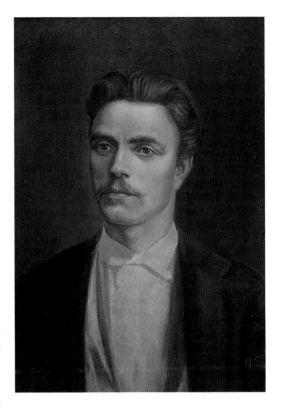

A portrait of the 'Apostle of Freedom' Vassil Levsky

Vasil Levsky's hiding place in Etropole Monastery in Stara Planina Range

Lyuben Karavelov's native house-museum in the town of Koprivsh-titsa. He was the ideologist of Bulgarian national revolution, leader of 'Bulgarian Central Revolutionary Committee', publicist, writer and student of folklore

Lyuben Karavelov's printing press on which the newspapers 'Freedom' and 'Independence' were printed

A monument of Lyuben Karavelov in the town of Koprivshtitsa

ond Bulgarian Legion was formed, which was disbanded by the Serb government. Legionaries went to Rumania and joined the detachment of Hadji Dimitar and Stefan Karadja (AD 1868). Crossing the Danube into Bulgaria this small battle formation (127 rebels) fought heavy battles along its entire march from the Danube to Stara Planina Range against the many times superior Turkish forces. Only a couple of people survived as if by a miracle; those that were taken captives were executed or sentenced to exile for life. Most often Bulgarians had been sent to Diarbekir, a town in the interior of Asia Minor which had become a synonym of isolation, sufferings and almost certain death. After that unfortunate AD 1868, a turn started in the revolutionary circles related to ideas and activity of Vasil Levsky and Lyuben Karavelov who captivated the radical forces among emigrants and in Bulgaria proper.

Vasil Kounchev (AD 1837-1873), known also as 'Levsky' and 'The Apostle', was born in the town of Karlovo. Ordained as monk while still a youth, in AD 1862 he cast off the cassock and joined Rakovsky's Legion. In AD 1867 was the standard-bearer in Panayot Hitov's detachment, in AD 1868 joined the Second Legion. Levsky sought a new way in which '… if I win, that means the entire nation wins; if I lose, I lose only myself…' The Apostle was deeply convinced that a successful uprising is possible only after a period of orderly internal preparation. From the end of AD 1868 till his capture by the end of 1872, he set up scores of revolutionary committees in towns and villages all over Bulgarian land. Their highest concentration was on both sides of Stara Planina Range but the plan envisaged to expand the network by setting up similar structures everywhere in Moesia, Thrace and Macedonia.

The poet-revolutionary Hristo Botyov's native house-museum in the town of Kalofer

The monument of Hristo Botyov in his native town of Kalofer

Among the emigration the leading position was held by Lyuben Karavelov (AD 1834-1879), an intellectual and an author who was under the influence of radical organizations in Russia and Europe. In Bucharest, Karavelov started publishing the newspaper 'Svoboda' (Freedom), a forum of the revolutionary wing of the emigration. Around Karavelov formed a circle of revolutionary figures, which transformed itself later into a 'Bulgarian revolutionary central committee' (BRCC). Levsky and his adherents in Bulgaria built up "Internal revolutionary organization' with its centre in the town of Lovech and connected with BRCC. In April-May 1872 in Bucharest was convened a general assembly of BRCC, which adopted a program and a statute. These proclaimed the self-dependence of Bulgarian revolution, 'a moral one and an armed one'. The purpose was to build up a democratic parliamentary state, according to what Levsky had once said, 'an unblemished and sacred republic'. Unfortunately, by the end of AD 1872 Vasil Levsky was captured at the outskirts of the village Kakrina not far from Lovech, put on trial, sentenced to death and hanged on February 6/18, 1873. The organization was seized by contradictions and hesitation. Attempts at finding a new chief apostle able to replace Levsky failed. Karavelov withdrew and in the circles of emigration it was Botev who was acknowledged as the new leader.

The genius poet and revolutionary Hristo Botev (AD 1848-1876) was the son of the well-known teacher Botyo Petkov. He studied in Odessa and in AD 1867 he found himself in Bucharest. The young Botev was captivated by the rebel atmosphere reining among the poor emigration (the so-called 'hushove' which means 'exiles' or 'outcasts'), wrote fiery poetry, published the newspaper 'Duma na balgarskite emigranti' (The Say of Bulgarian emigrants) (AD 1871), then became the closest assistant to Lyuben Karavelov. The uprising in Bosnia and Herzegovina in the summer of AD 1875 motivated BRCC to declare an uprising in its turn. Given the poor preparatory work and rashness an attempt at uprising was made only in Stara Zagora where the apostle was Stefan Stambolov. Authorities made arrests followed by repressions and executions. The failure made the emigration circles to explode: Botev submitted his resignation and BRCC went to pieces.

THE APRIL EPOPEE (AD 1876) AND THE LIBERATION OF BULGARIA

The decision on 'desperate revolution' was taken by the so-called 'Apostles committee" which sat by the end of AD 1875 in the town of Gyurgevo (Rumania). Members of this Committee were the youngest and most radical revolutionaries. By their decision they divided the country into 4 revolutionary districts. The basis in structuring these districts was the network of committees set up by Levsky. The aim had been to organize a large-scale uprising in May 1876.

The preparation was most enthusiastic in the Fourth (Plovdiv) district with its centre in the small town of Panagyurishte. Chief Apostle there was Panayuot Volov but his assistant Georgi Benkovski imposed his will and he himself became a leader. In the other three districts the preparation run against obstacles related to the lack of arms and the vigilance of authorities. On April 14, 1876 Benkovsky and Volov convened a people's assembly at the countryside area Oborishte. The assembly made fateful decisions, one on premature-

Monument of Georgi Benkovsky, commander of the Flying Detachment, one of the chief participants in April Uprising in AD 1876. The monument was erected on an elevation above his native town of Koprivshtitsa

A mausoleum in the town of Koprivshtitsa dedicated to the participants in April Uprising

Monument of Todor Kableshkov, the man who announced the April Uprising in AD 1876. Town of Koprivshtitsa

Ambassadors of the 'Great Powers' at Tsarigrad (Istanbul) Conference in AD 1876 (in the centre of the photo are Sir Henry Elliot and Graf Ignatief). The Conference worked out an 'Organizational Statutes' on the autonomy of Bosnia, Herzegovina and Bulgaria by which Bulgarian lands were separated into Eastern and Western Bulgaria by a vertical division line.

The church-museum in the town of Batak, a reminder of atrocities perpetrated by Turks during suppression of the April Uprising in AD 1876

ly starting the uprising if there was a risk of betrayal. Though somewhat belatedly, the authorities obtained information on the events under preparation and tried to arrest the organizers. Then Todor Kableshkov declared the uprising prematurely in Koprivshtitsa (20 April/1 May 1876). This was followed by the 'capital' Panagyurishte and scores of other settlements. Bulgarians started to fortify their villages and small towns, to pitch camps in the mountains but the adversary possessed smashing superiority. Against the primitive rifles and improvised wooden cannons (the so-called 'cherry-tree cannons') Turks used the most modern arms. Against Bulgarians were thrown both regular army and the marauding bands of the so-called Bashibozouk. Panagyurishte, the fortified camp Eledzhik, Perushtitsa, Bratzigovo and scores of other villages were drowned in blood… The most terrifying were the atrocities perpetrated in Batak - a public-spirited little town in Rodopi Mountains, which shook the world public.

In Tarnovo (First) district the uprising was parried by measures taken by the authorities. Only a couple of villages rose in arms (Kravenik, Novo Selo, Batoshevo); the big detachments of pop (*meaning 'parish priest'*) Hariton, Tsanko Dyustabanov and Hristo Patrev were called to the colours. The rebellion was drowned in blood, captured 'comitas' were executed or exiled. In the Second Revolutionary District (Sliven) the detachment led by Stoil Voyvode came out in arms; the ensuing massacre perpetrated by the Turks was most atrocious in the village of Boyadzhik, district of Yambol. In Vratsa (Third) district the weak revolutionary forces were paralyzed. The brightest event there was the heroic march of Botev's detachment, which crossed the Danube on board of the Austrian excursion steamship 'Radetzky' from Rumania. The poet-revolutionary perished in Stara Planina Range on June 2, 1876. Today June 2 is celebrated as a Day dedicated to those that have fallen for the freedom of Bulgaria.

In Macedonia the April epopee had its projection in the so-called Razlog uprising. In AD 1876 other detachments also entered Bulgaria, like those led by the Voyvodes Tanyu Stoyanov, Sider Grancharov, Todor Velkov. Thousands of men from the emigration in Rumania and Russia, which failed to take part in the uprising, joined the units that fought the Turks in the Serbian-Turkish conflict.

After the bloody suppression of April uprising a wave of protests flooded Europe, and 'atrocities in Bulgaria' were on the first pages of the world press. A voice in defense of Bulgarians raised the brightest figures of that epoch: Darwin, Hugo, Dostoevsky, Tolstoy, Turgenev, Garibaldi, the US journalist McGahan… This time the Great Powers could not ignore Bulgaria cause. The ambassadors' conference convened by the end of 1876 in the Turkish capital found a relatively acceptable by all solution: to set up two Bulgarian autonomous regions, East one with capital Tarnovo and Western one with capital Sofia. Turkish government rejected the plan. Only the path of war remained opened, which in the specific moment coincided with Russia's interests.

The war was declared on April 12/24 1877 in Kishinev by Emperor Alexander's II manifest. Bulgarian volunteers' corps formed a part of Russian army. Initially it was considered an

The big Russian monument on the mountain summit of St. Nikola; AD 1881; National Park-museum 'Shipka'.

The monument standing on the mountain summit Shipka where in August 1877 Bulgarian volunteer corps and some Russian battle units held back the advance of the army led by Suleiman Pasha the Magnificent

auxiliary force to execute secondary tasks and missions. On June 10/22 Russian soldiers set foot on Bulgarian land at the town of Machin in Northern Dobrudzha (today in Rumania). The main blow was at Svishtov on June 15/27. Russian forces operated in three detached forces: the Eastern, the Western and the Advanced Detachment. The volunteer corps was part of the Front detachment, which was under the command of Gen. Gurko and was the least numerous one (only 12 000-strong). The Volunteers' Corps was initially 7200 strong. Gurko penetrated impetuously into the south, freed the old capital of Tarnovo, crossed the Balkan range and captured Kazanlak, Stara Zagora and Nova Zagora. Suleiman Pasha set out against Gurko with a 40 000-strong army. The Russian-Bulgarian units were to withhold

A monument of 'Tsar Liberator' (Russian Emperor Alexander II) in Sofia. Work of the Florentine Arnaldo Dzochi; AD 1907

The temple-monument 'St Alexander Nevsky' in Sofia erected in honour of the fallen for the Liberation of Bulgaria and later proclaimed Patriarchate cathedral

the mountain pass of Shipka by all means. There, between August 9/21 and 13/25, 1877 was fought the most dramatic battle in the entire war. Only five thousand Russians and Bulgarians, almost without ammunitions repulsed Suleiman's attacks, and this to a large degree decided the outcome of the war.

The gross mistakes Russian high command had allowed were the cause of another big drama: Pleven, which was turned by Osman Ghazi Pasha into a storm-proof fortress. The three at-

tacks conducted by Rumanians and Russians were fruitless, thousand of lives were sacrificed. Only with the arrival of the experienced strategist Gen. Todtleben the besieged Pleven fell (November 16/28 1877). Gen. Gurko crossed the Balkan Range and seized Sofia (January 4, 1878). Turkish forces were utterly defeated at Shipka-Sheinovo and Plovdiv; Odrin also fell (January 14/26). Turkey begged for truce and on February 19/March 3 1878 the historical San Stefano Peace Treaty was signed.

FREE BULGARIA IN MODERN EUROPE

The fact that a state like San Stefano Bulgaria, with its surface area and potential emerged on the political map of Europe was badly undesired by the then Great Powers. The Berlin Congress convened in the summer of 1878 tore Bulgarian lands into 5 parts: the vassal principality of Bulgaria; the autonomous region of Eastern Rumelia; Macedonia and Thrace remained under the Ottoman rule; Rumania was given Northern Dobrudzha, while Serbia, Bulgarian Pomoravie (the valley of river Morava) with the towns of Nish, Vranya and Pirot.

Building up the institutions of the new state had started while the Liberation War was still under way and this was done by the so-called Interim Russian government. For geo-political reasons Sofia was chosen

A portrait of Alexander Batemberg (AD 1857-1893), a German Prince proclaimed in AD 1879 as Knyaz (Prince) of 'Principality of Bulgaria'

Knyaz Alexander Batemberg's mausoleum in Sofia, built up while he was still living and never used: in AD 1886 the Knyaz was forced to abdicate and left Bulgaria never to return again

to become the country capital. The spiritual unity of the nation continued to be personified by the Exarchate, the centre of which remained in the Turkish capital. On February 10, 1879, in the historical capital Tarnovo a constituent assembly was convened, consisting of 229 delegates from Moesia, Thrace and Macedonia. Their protest against the Berlin dictates did not bring any changes to the Great Powers' stand. After heated debates on April 16, 1879 the Tarnovo Constitution, one of the most democratic in Europe in that time, was voted. The Principality of Bulgaria was to be a constitutional monarchy with parliamentary government. The

German Prince Alexander Batemberg (1857-1893), a nephew of the Russian Empress was elected Prince (Knyaz) of Bulgaria. Two political trends formed: of the so-called Russophiles and Russophobes but the European vision of building up the social, state and cultural model dominated.

The first Bulgarian government with the Conservative Todor Bourmov (June 5, 1879) at the head was appointed by the Parliament. The initial steps of the young state were taken with impressive speed, not known in the Balkans. The constitution of the autonomous Eastern Rumelia with its capital Plovdiv was similar to that of the principality. Though 'de jure' it was part of the Ottoman Empire, Eastern Rumelia was being built up as a second Bulgarian Principality. The attempts made by the great Powers to present the region as a multiethnic one ended with complete fiasco: the elections for the Regional Assembly demonstrated in a most explicit way its entirely Bulgarian nature. In the Principality and in Eastern Rumelia sprang up the committees called 'Edinstvo' (Unity).

During the autumn and winter of 1878-1879 the Kresna-Razlog uprising broke out in Macedonia. It was severely suppressed by Turkish authorities. In spite of the unfavourable international situation Bulgarians

The house where in AD 1879 the 'Constitutional Assembly' held its sessions

The 'Tarnovo Constitution' adopted by the first Grand National Assembly; AD 1879

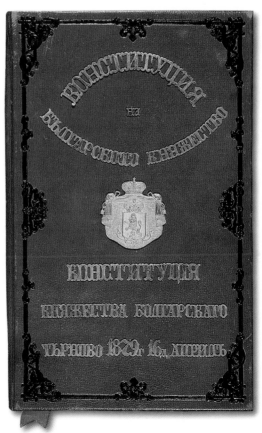

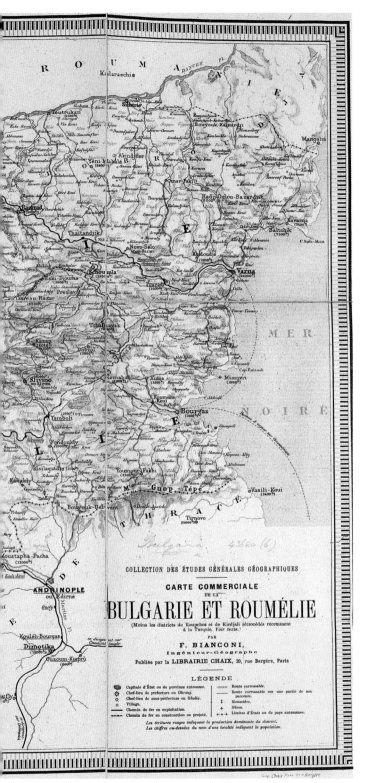

'Organization Statutes' of Eastern Rumelia; Plovdiv, AD 1879

The name of the autonomous region 'Eastern Rumelia' had been borrowed from 'Rumily', a name with which the Ottomans designated their European possessions after 14th century AD. It is rooted in the Iranian (Persian) 'Rum' meaning Rome (the Roman Empire actually). The region of 'Eastern Rumelia' is a fabricated term which, apart from anything else, shows up in the fact that not a single European or Russian diplomat has never determined where the respective counterpart, the 'Western Rumelia', should be located

A trader's map of 'Bulgaria and Rumelia'. By F. Bianconi; AD 1888

Todor Bourmov, prime-minister of the first Bulgarian government of Principality of Bulgaria. Sofia; AD 1879

Knyaz (Prince) Alexander Bo- goridy, Governor-general of Eastern Rumelia. Plovdiv; AD 1879

Knyaz (Prince) Ferdinand Saxe- Coburg-Gotha. Proclaimed ruling Prince of 'Principality of Bulgaria' in AD 1887 (from AD 1908, pro- claimed Tsar of Bulgaria)

from Eastern Rumelia aspired after unit- ing with the Principality. Even the Governor General Alexander (Aleko) Bogoridi and Gavril Krastevich tacitly encouraged these moods. A Bulgarian Secret Central Revolu- tionary Committee (BSCRC) was set up in Plovdiv with the apostle from the April ep- opee, the vehement political journalist and writer Zahary Stoyanov as a chair. BSCRC had as its goal the liberation of Macedonia and Thrace but the only realistic possibili- ty was the unification of Rumelia with the Principality. On September 6, 1885 the Com- mittee members declared the Unification as a fact. They had the full support of the army and the people.

The violation of the Berlin pact gave pre- text to Serbia to attack Bulgaria. The young Bulgarian army, although lacking senior of- ficers defeated the aggressor with its reso- lute and vigorous actions. 'The war of cap- tains' astounded Europe. Russia's negative attitude towards the unification caused em- bitterment among Bulgarians while Eng- land, Germany and Austria-Hungary sur-

prisingly acknowledged the act. On August 9, 1885 a group of officers of pro-Russian orientation made a coup. National forces led by the chair of the People's Assembly, Stefan Stambolov, neutralized the mutiny. Prince Alexander was restored to the throne but the irreconcilability of Petersburg turned into hysteria… In August 1886 the Prince abdicated. Chief figure in the regents' coun- cil was Stambolov. After rude but unsuc- cessful intervention Russia broke off diplo- matic relations with Bulgaria and provoked the so-called 'mutinies of the officers-Rus- sophiles' in Rousse and Silistra (February 1887), which were quickly suppressed. On June 25, 1887 the Third Grand National As- sembly elected Prince Ferdinand Saxe-Co- burg-Gotha (1861-1948) for Knyaz (Prince) of Bulgaria. Russia did not acknowledge the election. Western states abstained from di- rect contacts with the new monarch but in fact 'Bulgarian crisis' was over.

THE ROAD TO INDEPENDENCE

Ferdinand I entrusted the government to the most powerful political figure in the country: Stefan Stambolov (1854-1895). The Prime Minister personified the decisive change in Bulgarian foreign policy conditioned by the very development of the young state. The efforts to catch up with the leading European states and the defense of national interests (liberation of Macedonia included) were unimaginable without sweeping and profound modernization. Thanks to the governmental protectionism, attraction of foreign capitals, etc. the factory industry marked considerable growth. Construction of the ports at Varna and Bourgas started; the road and railway network was developing; in 1888 the Higher School (Sofia University) was opened.

Bulgaria was coming out of international isolation. The policy regarding the 'national question' was focused on education and church, on preservation of the spiritual unity of nation divided between the freed and still enslaved lands. Stambolov held a firm position regarding the indivisibility of Macedonia.

The iron will of Stambolov, the complexity of the tasks, and the still non-matured Bulgarian democracy inevitably led to the implementation of the 'firm hand' policy. The discontent from 'Stambolov's regime' united his political adversaries. Knyaz Ferdinand tacitly joined their camp but still remaining in the shadow of the dictator. On May 18, 1894 Stambolov fell from power, and Konstantin Stoilov, leader of the People's Party

Stefan Stambolov, prime-minister of Bulgaria, AD 1887-1894

The government of Dr. Constantine Stoilov in front of the National Assembly building. Sofia; AD 1898

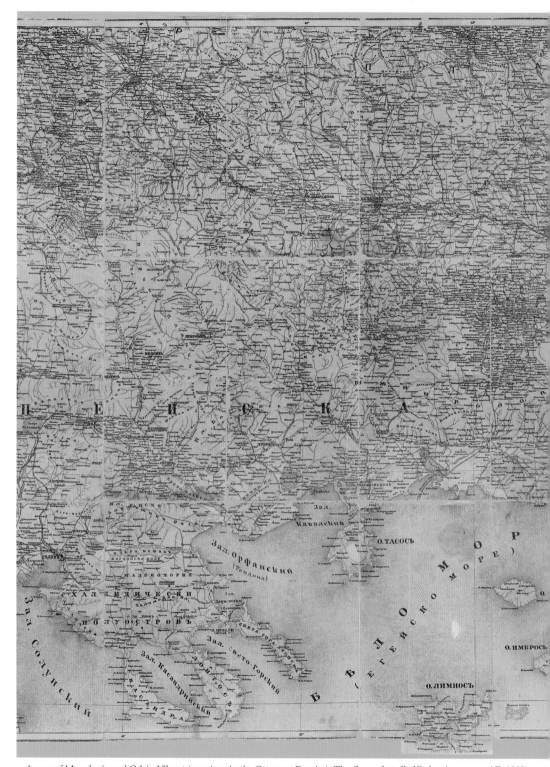

A map of Macedonia and Odrin Vilayet (province in the Ottoman Empire). The General staff of Bulgarian army; AD 1902

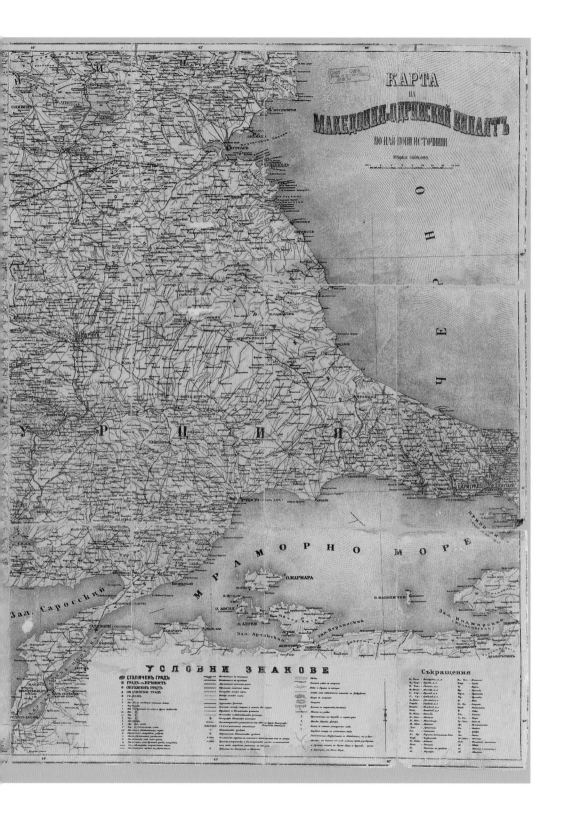

85

A factory for manufacturing wool textile products built up by Evlogy Georgiev for the benefit of his home town of Karlovo; AD 1891

The building of Sofia University 'St Kliment Ohridsky' built up with funds and property donated by Bulgarian large-scale businessmen, the brothers Evlogy and Hristo Georgiev

was appointed Prime Minister. A year after that 'Bulgarian Bismark' was assassinated by hired assassins… Bulgaria had lost one of its greatest statesmen.

In 1896 Ferdinand was recognized as the lawful Prince by Petersburg but the mutual trust was not restored. The world agricultural crisis in the beginning of 20th century affected Bulgaria too. The country stabilized under the so-called 'Second Stambolovist's regime' (1903-1908). One of the top priorities was to build up a modern army, which in-

spired respect not only in the country's Balkan neighbours but also in European governments. The vassal position of the country did not correspond to its real position in international politics. On September 22, 1908, in the old capital of Tarnovo Bulgaria was declared an independent state and Ferdinand, 'tsar of Bulgarians'.

THE CAPTIVE BULGARIAN LAND: MACEDONIA

The development of free Bulgaria was hampered by the decisions of the Berlin Congress, which had tore the nation's unity, making at the same time the fate of the 'enslaved brothers' a painful issue to entire Bulgarian society. The national issue gradually concentrated onto Macedonia where Bulgarians made up about 70% of the population. Bulgaria made possible endeavours to develop education and school network as well as the church institutions in Macedonia. The role the Exarchate played, with the authoritative Josef I at its head, was of fundamental importance. In the fight against the Greek Patriarchate, the Turkish authorities, the Serbian and

A portrait of Exarch Josef I who was at the head of Bulgarian Exarchate (AD 1877-1915) and was the embodiment of the national unity of Bulgarians from Moesia, Thace and Macedonia

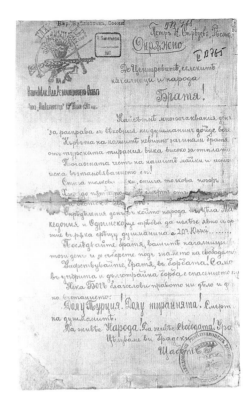

A proclamation of the Chief staff of Bitola revolutionary district. By this proclamation the Ilinden-Preobrazhenie Uprising was declared, which broke out in Odrin Thrace and Macedonia on July 15, 1903

Greek 'propaganda' Bulgarians built up church institutions, high schools in Solun (Salonika) and Odrin (*Edirne in today's Turkey*), nearly thousand town and village schools with 1500 teachers and scores of thousands of schoolchildren.

The revolutionary movement developed also in the spirit of the National Revival traditions. In 1893, the Bulgarian Macedonian-Odrin Revolutionary Committee (BMORC) was set up in Solun. Its first chairman was Dr. Hristo Tatarchev. It was an organization known more by its subsequent name of Internal Macedonian-Odrin Revolutionary Organization or by its abbreviation IMORO. The example after which IMORO was organized was Levsky's committees and its leader Georgi (Gotse) Delchev (1872-1903) was perceived as the new 'Apostle of Freedom'. Damian (Dame)

Leaders of IMORO (Internal Macedonian-Odrin Revolutionary Organization):

Dame (Damian Grouev): the man who set up the first IMORO committees

Gotse (Georgi) Delchev: a representative abroad and chief commanding officer for the IMORO detachments

Gyorche Petrov: a member of IMORO Central Committee

Michael Gerdzhikov: leader of the Odrin (Thracian) revolutionary organization

Gruev (1871-1906), the other great organizer of IMORO, was setting up the revolutionary committees and reading to Bulgarians passages from the book 'Memoirs on Bulgarian uprisings' by Zahary Stoyanov… Taking into consideration the position of the Great Powers, a tactical goal was set before the organization: to achieve autonomy of Macedonia and the region of Odrin which, at some later time to unite with Bulgaria as did Eastern Rumelia before. In 1895 in Sofia was established the Supreme Macedonian-Odrin Committee with connections to the Palace and the army. Despite some disagreements in opinion, between the two organizations existed close collaboration.

In view of the stiffening Turkish repressions, in the summer of 1903 the Ilinden-Preobrazhenie uprising burst out. The rebels operations were doomed in the face of the crushing preponderance of the enemy. The international situation was unfavourable. Russia and Austria-Hungary warned Bulgaria not to intervene. Thousands of victims fell; over 200 Bulgarian villages were set to fire and burnt to ashes; thousands of refugees sought rescue in Bulgaria. It was becoming increasingly clear that the national issue would not be solved by an uprising, nor by diplomatic steps, nor by ostensible 'reforms' promised by the Empire.

THE WARS FOR NATIONAL UNIFICATION (1912-1918)

Political processes in the beginning of the 20th century prognosticated an inevitable war with the Ottoman Empire for the liberation of the enslaved lands. In 1912 the so-called Balkan Alliance with Serbia, Greece and Montenegro was founded. The Russophile government of Ivan Evstatiev Geshov departed from the principle of indivisibility of Macedonia. The most important task of the war to come was the strategic attack towards Tsarigrad (Istanbul), which was entirely and fully a responsibility of Bulgarian army. However, most of Bulgarians under the Ottoman rule lived in Macedonia, and there the military operations were assigned to Serbia and Greece.

On October 5, 1912 the Balkan War broke out. It was regarded by the entire Bulgarian society as a liberation war. Within only a couple of months Bulgarian troops defeated the enemy reaching the Sea of Marmara and the avenues of approach to the Turkish capital! Thanks to the talent of the commanding officers as well as to the unprecedented bravery of Bulgarian soldiers, the fortified, and declared as a 'storm-proof', city of Odrin fell. Serbs and Greeks achieved success in Macedonia, Epirus, and Thessaly where the resistance was far weaker. With the London peace treaty (May 17, 1913) the allies received all lands to the west of the line Mydia-Enos (*these are two towns in Eastern Thrace, one on the Black Sea, the other on the White /Aegean/ Sea coasts*). Greece and Serbia concluded a surreptitious alliance against Bulgaria. In spite of the agreed 'indisputable zone' Serbian invaders subjected Macedonian Bulgarians to repressions. Hopes for a fair arbitration on the part of Russian Emperor proved

Bulgarian airplane that did the first in history air bombing on October 18, 1912 (over Odrin fortress)

The torpedo boat 'Drazky': during the first Balkan War in AD 1912 torpedoed the Turkish cruiser 'Hamidie'. Today it stands as a naval museum in Varna seaside garden

Odrin fortress after it was captured by Bulgarian army. The picture was taken on March 15, 1912

Field Marshal von Mackensen and the commanding officers of the individual Bulgarian armies. Town of Kyustendil

Tsar Ferdinand (wearing Austrian uniform of a field marshal), Emperor Carl I of Austria (in Bulgarian uniform of a general) and the chief commanding officer of the operative army Gen. Nicola Zhekov. Town of Kyustendil

groundless. Serbian and Greek provocations accompanied by ubiquitous overexcitement in Bulgaria led to the fatal June 16, 1913. Bulgarian troops rebuffed actions deliberately carried out by the allies but before the European public Bulgaria was presented as a violator of peace! Soon Bulgarian army moved on to counter-offensive, threatening Greek forces with utter defeat. Most unexpectedly, Rumanian army rushed across the Danube. In its turn Turkey occupied Eastern Thrace putting local Bulgarians to bloody outrages and massacres! The treacherous blow carried out with the implicit consent of Russia forced Bulgaria to surrender. The attempt at national unification ended with a catastrophe and bare-faced robbery of Bulgarian lands by its neighbours.

Thousands of soldiers' monuments scattered all over Bulgarian lands remind to the generations of the dear victims given during the wars for national unification

A monument dedicated to those that had fallen in the wars AD 1912-1918 in the village of Svidnya, district of Sofia

A monument of those that had fallen in the wars AD 1912-1918 in the town of Kyustendil

A monument of the perished residents of the town of Kalofer in the wars AD 1915-1918, town of Kalofer

The Monument of the Unknown Soldier in Sofia erected in front of the southern wall of the ancient church 'St Sofia'. It is a tomb with a sarcophagus and 5 stone urns with bones of soldiers that have fallen for Bulgaria; also soil from all four corners of the country was brought here. On a round bronze altar standing on four swords an eternal flame is burning and to the left is the sculpture of a bronze lion. On a massive stone slab decorated by two laurel wreaths the following verses by the famous Bulgarian poet Ivan Vazov were chiseled out:

> *"Bulgaria, for you they died,*
> *You only were deserving their sacrifice*
> *And they deserved you, Mother!"*

The unsolved national issue pre-determined the participation of Bulgaria on the side of the Central Forces. In 1915-1918 Bulgarian army achieved remarkable victories over Rumania, Greece and Serbia, against British and French units at the Solun front and against the Russian units in Dobrudzha: the battles at Kosovo Pole, at Tutrakan, Dobrich, Doiran Lake, etc. are even today a model of the art of war and wonders of valour. Given the insufficient resources of the country, the trench warfare proved beyond the country endurance... In the autumn of 1918 the forces of the Entente, with their preponderance managed to break Bulgarian defense at Dobro Pole. Large groups of soldiers set out on their way to Sofia to seek retribution... Their discontent was incited by the populism of the agrarian party BZNS (standing for Bulgarian Agrarian People's Union) and by the activities of the increasingly turning 'Bolshevik' after the example of the Russian October revolution Bulgarian Workers' Social-Democratic Party (left-wing socialists or communists). The mutineers were defeated but the capitulation was inevitable. After more than thirty years of reigning Ferdinand abdicated in favour of his son Boris III (1894-1943).

Grave and humiliating treaties were imposed on the defeated ones at Paris peace conference in November 1919. According to the Neuilly treaty (November 27, 1919) Serbia seized the Western Outlying Parts; Greece seized Western Thrace by which Bulgaria was deprived of White (Aegean) Sea outlet. Within the reduced state borders moved more than 400 thousand refugees. Severe reparations were imposed; the army was reduced to small-numbered volunteer corps, without aviation, tanks and modern arms. This catastrophe was the most painful wound to Bulgarian national psychology in the 20th century.

BULGARIA BETWEEN THE TWO WORLD WARS

On the one hand, the national tragedy toppled the 'old political parties', and on the other hand the social schemes of agrarians and communists radicalized society. BZNS (Bulgarian Agrarian People's Union) with Alexander Stamboliysky at the head came to power (1920). Daring reforms were carried out which, irrespective of the elements of social justice, affected negatively in most of the cases the national economy. The government domestic and foreign policy created significant tension in the society. The dissatisfaction pervaded all political powers: from the rightist parties and the revolutionaries from VMRO (*standing for Internal Macedonian Revolutionary Organization*) to the communists. The elements of 'peasant dictatorship' provoked Bulgarian officers' corps, the Military Union of which made a military coup d'etat on June 9, 1923. BZNS' adherents, and at places the anarchists and

The building of the Ministry for War in Sofia. Designed by architect D. Tsolov; AD 1938

communists rose in spontaneous revolts, quickly suppressed by the army. The new government with Prof. Alexander Tsankov at the head was detached by the Democratic

The building of the Ministry for Agriculture in Sofia. Designed by architect N. Lazarov, finished by architect Il. Popov; AD 1924

The building of hotel Imperial in Sofia. Designed by architect K. Marichkov; AD 1920

The church 'St Nedelya' in Sofia destroyed by the bloody terrorist act in AD 1925

Tsar Boris III coming ashore from a boat at the port of Vasilico (today's Tsarevo) on the occasion of its official opening; AD 1939

A postcard 'In memory of the royal wedding of Their Majesties Tsar Boris III and Tsarina Ioanna"; AD 1930

Accord, a new formation which had united some of the older parties.

Under the dictate of Soviet Russia the communists took a line towards revolution. The so-called September Uprising broke out (1923). The operations of rebels were poorly coordinated being most concentrated in the North-Western Bulgaria. The violence reverberated dramatically on Bulgarian society; democratic traditions were shaken. In 1925 communists organized a terrorist act in the cathedral St Nedelya in Sofia: one of the bloodiest such acts in the 20th century in the entire world. Authorities in turn responded with repressions and political murders.

During the rule of the People's Bloc (1931-1934) the democratic model was restored. The spur in economy was somewhat handicapped by the global financial crisis. The foreign policy pursued 'peaceful revisionism' and overcoming the restrictive clauses of the Neuilly treaty. Authoritarian trends were materialized by the military coup d'etat on May 19, 1934, by which all political parties were outlawed. Tsar Boris III took advantage of the internal conflicts among the military, removed the so-called '19-May people' and established his personal regime. The experienced diplomat Georgi Kyoseivanov became prime minister. The country followed a line of non-alignment with the Great Powers. Bulgaria maintained intensive trade relations with the Third Reich, which had a most favourable effect on the industry and agriculture.

BULGARIA IN THE SECOND WORLD WAR (1939-1945)

At the commencement of the World War II Bulgaria fell into the political orbit of Germany. With its support a serious diplomatic success was achieved: Rumania was compelled to hand back Southern Dobrudzha (1940). Policy of neutrality was increasingly harder to keep. Tsar Boris III and the government of Prof. Bogdan Filov were put to pressure both from Moscow and from Berlin. When the Balkans became a theatre of war, Prime-Minister Filov was forced to sign the act of joining the Axis (Rome, Berlin and Tokyo (March 1, 1941), though without a clause on taking part in military operations. After Germany occupied Yugoslavia and Greece Bulgaria was given to administer part of its original lands: the Western Outlying Parts with the town of Pirot, Vardar Macedonia and the Belomorie (White /Aegean/ Sea Coastal Thrace). Everywhere Bulgarian troops were met with indescribable enthusiasm by the local population; Tsar Boris III was named the 'Unifier'.

The onset of Germany against Soviet Union (June 22, 1941) stirred up Bulgarian communists who began an armed struggle against the government. Under German dictate Bulgaria declared symbolical war to USA and Great Britain (December 12, 1941), an act which provoked bombing on the part of allies and was paid by Bulgarians with sacrifice of life, destruction and international isolation. However, the peace and diplomatic relations with USSR were preserved: a phenomenon indeed on the background of the escalation of military operations at the Eastern front. In Bulgaria the Nazi doctrine for genocide on Jews was utterly unpopular. German occupational forces deported 11 thousand Jews from Macedo-

The monument of Bulgarian fighter-pilot. It stands in the garden between National Assembly building and Sofia University building, erected in AD 1941 by the Academic Flying Club on behalf of the university students. It is the first art work by the sculptor Georgi Kotsev

University students-members of R.M.S. (Young Workers Union or YWU) welcome the Soviet troops with a placard which reads "Eternal glory to the Red Army!"

The monument in memory of the Soviet Army invasion, erected in the city of Plovdiv in AD 1956

nia and the White Sea Coastal Thrace. Bulgarian society stood in defense of the 50 thousand Bulgarian Jews, most of whose descendants live today in Israel.

Guided from Moscow, Bulgarian Communist Party (BCP) built up a coalition with other opposition parties: the so-called Fatherland Front (FF). The sudden death of Tsar Boris (August 28, 1943), the successes of the Red Army, and of the Allies in Italy and at the Western Front in 1944 made Bulgaria to face a grave drama. The attempts at contacts with Great Britain and USA failed. A government of the legal opposition was formed on September 2, 1944 with Constantine Mouraviev as Prime Minister. The efforts for re-orientating the country to the anti-Hitler coalition and the restoration of democracy were spoiled by the Soviet Union by its declaring war to Bulgaria (September 5, 1944) without any pretext given by the latter. In Sofia, military units perpetrated a coup on behalf of the Fatherland Front. On September 9, 1944 a government was formed with Kimon Georgiev at the head but the levers of power were in the hands of communists.

95

BULGARIAN CULTURE
(1878 – 1944)

The Liberation led to a growth in the qualitative aspect of culture, to Bulgaria coming closer to the European traditions and contemporariness. During the first decades the powerful talent of the 'people's poet' Ivan Vazov (1850-1921) dominated Bulgarian culture. The first Bulgarian novel recreating the atmosphere of the April Uprising had become renowned all over the world. The literary and public presence of Petko R. Slaveykov, Zahary Stoyanov, Stoyan Mihaylovsky, Aleko Konstantinov, Elin Pelin was also powerful. By the end of the 19th and the beginning of the 20th century the ideas of the European symbolism entered Bulgarian culture and found their expression in the works of Pencho Slaveykov, Peyo Yavorov, Nikolay Liliev, Dimcho Debelyanov.

The wars and the political concussions that followed gave birth to new artistic trends in the creative work of Yordan Yovkov, Anton Strashimirov, Theodore Trajanov, Georgi Raychev, Constantine Constantinov, Chavdar Mutafov, etc. Hristo Smirnensky, Geo Milev and Nikola Vaptsarov formed a trend in which dominated the revolutionary and social involvement.

Monument of the classic of Bulgarian literature Ivan Vazov and his native house in the town of Sopot, district of Plovdiv

A corner dedicated to the memory of Ivan Vazov in the Cherepish Monastery near the village of Cherepish, district of Sofia. The veranda above river Iskar had been his favourite place for rest and work

A portrait of the writer Aleko Konstantinov (1863-1897), author of the emblematic literary character Bai Ganyo, a collective image of the newly emerging at that time (last quarter of the 19ᵗʰ century) Bulgarian bourgeois…

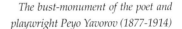

The bust-monument of the poet and playwright Peyo Yavorov (1877-1914)

Town of Koprivshtitsa, native house-museum of Dimcho Debelyanov, one of Bulgaria's most tender poets. He fell at the age of 29 on the battle-fields of the First World War. In the courtyard of the house, in the flower garden, visitors are met by the monument of poet's mother (AD 1934), a work of the talented Bulgarian sculptor Ivan Lazarov who had been inspired by the moving lyrics by the poet. The original was placed on the poet's grave in the courtyard of the church 'The Assumption' where, on the commemorative tablet resembling a town of Koprivshtitsa wooden gate, the following verses have been cut into the stone: "…and in a gentle languor waits she for her child to come…"

Slaveykov's house in the Balkan town of Tryavna. In this house the writer, enlightener and politician Petko Slaveykov had lived with his good-sized family. His sons Ivan, Racho, Hristo and Pencho were eminent publicists and public figures, some were politicians and statesmen; of them Pencho Slaveykov stands out as a poet, translator, essayist, nominated from Bulgaria for the Nobel Prize in literature with his poem 'A bleeding song'

National Theatre 'Ivan Vazov' in Sofia. Built up in AD 1907 after the design of architects Helmer and Felner from Vienna. Following a fire in 1923 the building was almost completely destroyed; it has been restored in its contemporary appearance after the design of Prof. Duelfer from Dresden

The building of the people's theatre in Bulgaria's sea capital Varna; erected in AD 1910 after the design of architect Lazarov

'Bulgarian Madonna', artist Vladimir Dimitrov-The Master-hand

'Old Plovdiv', AD 1938. Artist Tsankpo Lavrenov

'Night pasture, artist Zlatyu Boyadzhiev

The astronomic observatory. It was established as part of the Higher School (Sofia University) in AD 1894. The big telescope installed under the big dome in AD 1897 was the first in the Balkans and one of the biggest in Europe. It was manufactured in Ireland and was donated by Knyaz (Prince) Ferdinand I Saxe-Coburg-Gotha

Prof. Marin Bachvarov, founder of the Chair in Astronomy with the School of Physics and Mathematics of Sofia University 'St Kliment Ohridsky'

The building of Bulgarian Academy of Sciences in Sofia (constructed in AD 1892), reconstructed in AD 1926

Classical and modern trends have been imposed on Bulgarian pictorial and plastic arts after the Liberation (Ivan Mrkvichka, Anton Mitov). During the first decades of 20th century Tseno Todorov, Elisaveta Konsulova-Vazova, Alexander Bozhinov, Boris Georgiev, Alexander Mutafov, Andrey Nikolov and others became notable ion the artistic wold. The interpretation of the national theme in humanitarian spirit involved the creative quests of Yaroslav Veshin, Boris Denev, Ivan Lazarov. The postwar years formed the mature period in the creative work of Vladimir Dimitrov-The Master, Tsanko Lavrenov, Zlatyu Boyadzhiev, Dechko Ouzounov. Bulgarian theatre became stronger; directors began putting up plays by Yavorov, Racho Stoyanov, Stefan L. Kostov; Bulgarian cinema/movie industry made its first steps.

TOTALITARIAN SYSTEM (1944-1989)

The allocation of the spheres of influence between the victors in World War II placed Bulgaria in the Soviet Union's orbit.

Despite declarations in the democratic spirit, the new rulers took the law in their hands in a most cruel manner with regard to the fate of the cadres from the previous political regime. The height of cynicism was the so-called 'People's Court of Law'. Bulgaria was covered by a network of prisoners' camps, scores of thousands of Bulgarians perished.

Bulgaria took part in the final phase of the war against Germany giving more than thirty-eight thousand of victims. As early as with the armistice from the autumn of 1944 the country lost in fact its sovereignty. Backed by the USSR the communist dominated from the very beginning; each and every one of their opponents was doomed. The opposition headed by the leader of agrarians Nikola Petkov was annihilated in the period 1946-1947. On September 8, 1946, following a plebiscite, Bulgaria was declared 'People's Republic'. By manipulations and forgeries the communists, being at the head of the Fatherland Front, won overwhelming majority in the parliament. Prime Minister became Georgi Dimitrov (1882-1949), (*chair of the Comintern,* *an abbreviation standing for the 'communist international organization'*), who had just come back from Moscow after decades of absence from the country. The new (*Dimitrov's*) constitution established the full power of communists and the state monopoly in all aspects of life in the country (1947). One of the gravest crimes of Bulgarian Communist Party (BCP) was the recognition of 'Macedonian nation' for the convenience of Yugoslavian communists with Josip Broz Tito at the head. Not less dangerous was the intention of forming a federation with Yugoslavia. At the signing of the peace treaty with the states-victors in the World War II in Paris (February 10, 1947) Bulgaria was not recognized as a co-belligerent nation (even the Soviet Union did not make an exception from this stand!) – a fact that imposed on it reparations and unfavourable terms of peace.

The epoch of the 'Cold War' between the USSR and the West that had started in 1947, had made Bulgaria a part of the global communist experiment. A large-scale attack started against private property and free economic enterprise. The task of 'building up socialism' was set by the 5th congress of the BCP (December 1948). Thus started an accelerated industrialization of the country; the national economy

The Communist Party Central House. Today it is a part of Republic of Bulgaria's National Assembly complex

The monument of the Soviet Army in Sofia.

Bourgas: the square 'Troykata' with the monument of 'Alyosha' and the building that was erected to be the Communist Party House.

One of the buildings of the Government Residence in Sofia Borough of Boyana nowadays accommodates the National Museum of History

A chapel in the garden of the National Palace of Culture in memory of those persecuted by Bulgarian Communist Party (AD 1945-1989)

became fully dependent on the Soviet Union. Bulgaria joined the COMECON organization (the full name of which was Council on Mutual Economic Aid) and the Warsaw Pact (the military bloc set up as a counterpoise to NATO), which bound it politically, economically and militarily most of all to Moscow.

Stalin's formulations on 'aggravation of the class struggle' were in fact instructions on con-tinuing with the policy of coercion and outrage, over the Orthodox Church, Roman-Catholic priesthood, Protestants included. The repres-sions reached, in the natural course of events, to the 'enemy with Bulgarian Communist Party membership card': hundreds of party function-aries were arrested, tormented and sentenced to death or prison. Put to death was also the 'trai-tor' Traycho Kostov, one of the BCP leaders.

'THE APRIL EPOCH' OF TODOR ZHIVKOV

The death of Stalin on March 5, 1953 and the decisions taken by the 20th congress of CPSU (*standing for 'Communist Party of the Soviet Union'*) caused serious changes. Todor Zhivkov (1911-1998), elected first secretary of BCP's Central Committee, won Moscow's support and that of the BCP's Central Committee April Plenary Session (1956). The concept of 'peaceful co-existence' was a favourable condition for Bulgaria's foreign policy. Despite the dependency on USSR (the Brezhnev's doctrine' as called by western political scientists) Bulgaria developed its relations with Federal Republic of Germany, Japan and other countries. In relations with Yugoslavia Todor Zhivkov rejected the anti-national line

A demonstration in Sofia on the occasion of the 60th anniversary of the Great October Revolution. From left to right are the portraits of the members of Political bureau (Politbureau) of the Communist Party with Todor Zhivkov at the head, and the same of the Communist Party of the Soviet Union with Leonid Brezhnev at the head; November 7, 1977

The monument on the Stara Planina summit of Bouzloudzha erected in honour of some anniversary from constituting there, in AD 1891, Bulgarian Social-democratic Party (BSDP) later renamed to Bulgarian Communist Party (BCP)

A demonstration in Sofia on the occasion of May 24th, the Day of Bulgarian Enlighteners Cyril and Methodius and of the Slav Script. On platform of Georgi Dimitrov's Mausoleum stand Bulgaria's communist party and state leaders with Todor Zhivkov at the head

The ceremony of bestowing on Francois Miterand the title of Sofia University 'honoris causa doctor' in AD 1989

Students rally in front of Sofia University 'St Kliment Ohridsky' building, AD 1989

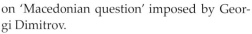

on 'Macedonian question' imposed by Georgi Dimitrov.

In 1971, the 10th BCP congress carried up the thesis of building up 'a developed socialist society'. This formulation entered the new constitution of the country according which a new supreme organ, the State Council, was formed, and Todor Zhivkov was elected head of state. The development of the 'socialist' economy reached its climax by introducing some elements of the free market economy, some new technologies, etc. This led to a certain improvement of the standard of living but as a whole the foreign indebtedness of the country increased. In 1980s a system of reforms was designed with elements of free market economy of the small-scale type (for instance the ill-famed in those years 'Decree No. 56'). One way or the other, the commanding-administrative system and the monopo-

ly of state together with the incompetence of the party nomenclature remained. Among the dramatic events of that time in Bulgaria was the so-called 'revival process' with respect to Bulgarian Turks. The political gridlock deepened in the summer of 1989 when three hundred and fifty thousand people emigrated in neighbouring Turkey.

The mid-1980s marked an aggravation of the negative trends in the economy not only of Bulgaria but also of the entire 'socialist camp'. After Brezhnev's death in 1982 the Soviet Union and the whole of the Soviet 'empire' fell into a permanent political instability. The 'perestroika' started by the CPSU leader Michael Gorbachov was in fact a foredoomed attempt at rescuing the system.

BULGARIAN CULTURE
(1944 – 1989)

The communist regime introduced cardinal changes in Bulgarian culture, too. The dogmas of the so-called 'socialist realism' struggled to transform the creative work of writers, poets and artists into a propaganda cliché but in the 1960s the literature and the fine art restored their national characteristics. Authors of value in the person of writers Dimitar Dimov, Dimitar Talev, Emiliyan Stanev, Yordan Radichkov, Ivaylo Petrov, Nikolay Haytov won recognition. Tolerated 'party' poets could not match in popularity workers like Atanas Dalchev, the rebel Penyo Penev, Valery Petrov, Konstantin Pavlov, Boris Hristov… Nedyalko Yordanov, Stefan Tsanev and others became widely known. Manifestations of free-thinking were met with approval by the broad public. Plays by Georgi Danailov and Stanislav Stratiev as well as a whole series of movies by talented directors became very popular in 1970s and 1980s. The creative work of artists like Iliya Petrov, Alexander Poplilov, Georgi Pavlov, Ivan Nenov, Marin Varbanov, Svetlin Roussev showed many European features. Bulgarian musicians won public recognition, particularly opera singers who conquered' world stages (Boris Hristov, Nikolay Gyaourov, Raina Kabaivanska, Gena Dimitrova, and quite a number more).

After the mid-1960s Bulgarian society was increasingly opening towards the influence of the culture of the West. Brutally banning the 'decadent' influence was rather fruitless. In the cultural processes of 1970s significant role was played by Lyudmila Zhivkova who carried through a more independent policy, especially towards cul-

The monument of St Kliment Ohridsky, one of the disciples of the saint borthers Cyril and Methodius, creators of the Slavonic script

The Monument 'Kambanite' (the Bells): a symbol of the international children's assembly 'Banner of Peace' held in Bulgaria on initiative of Lyudmila Zhivkova

A wall carpet 'Alafranghi G", by Marin Varbanov; 250cm x 800 cm, AD 1975. A monumental textile artwork with stylized images based on Bulgarian folklore and the historical tradition

National Library 'St Cyril and Methodius'; there the largest literary and documentary archive stock in Bulgaria from all fields of knowledge is kept. The building was erected in mid-20th century and was declared a monument of culture

National Palace of Culture, Sofia. At the 2003 competition for the best congress center, organized by the International Association of Congress Palaces it ranked second in the world

The poetess Blaga Dimitrova, Herder prize winner and vice-president of Republic of Bulgaria, and the writer and President of the Czech Republic - Vatslav Havel exchange their works, AD 1992

ture of the West, world movie making, modern music, teachings of the East. Gradually, the national theme in history, TV, radio, fine arts was reborn.

DEMOCRATIC BULGARIA AND UNITED EUROPE

In Bulgaria, due to various reasons, especially because of the total control exerted by the communist party organizations and the secret services (State Security), there were practically no dissenters' organizations. Only by the end of the period in question emerged an 'Independent Society for the Protection of Human Rights', 'Ecoglasnost' (*i.e. openness on environmental issues*), the independent workers' syndicate 'Podkrepa' (*Support*), etc. The dissatisfaction with Todor Zhivkov's 'personal rule' increased even within the elite circle of the higher party nomenclature. The 'First One' was forced to submit his resignation. The internal party take-over marked the end not only of Todor Zhivkov's rule but of the communist party rule in Bulgaria as well. Some of the old political parties were restored and new ones sprang up. Part of these formed the so-called Union of Democratic Forces (UDF), which became the chief opposition bloc to the communists. Under the pressure of the events Bulgarian Communist Party (BCP) gave up its ideology and even changed its name to Bulgarian Socialist Party (BSP).

During 1990s a pluralistic democratic system has been built up in Bulgaria. The country avoided the serious concussions that hit hard some of the former socialist countries in Eastern Europe and in the Balkans (especially former Yugoslavia). Bulgarian society demonstrated its high degree of maturity and its abilities for integrating into the modern world. The disintegration of the so-called socialist system and the reforms towards a market economy affected in a negative way the industrial sector of the national economy as well as the 'cooperative/collective' agriculture. The state proved to be a poor proprietor and the state-owned industrial enterprises turned into perfect ground for corruption and organized crime to increase tremendously. Reforms undertaken till the mid-1990s were half-way measures in-

A rally of the adherents and fans of Bulgarian Socialist Party (BSP), expressing the leftist ideas

A rally of the Union of the Democratic Forces (in Bulgarian SDS) who at that time expressed the rightist political ideas

The rite of relieving guard in front of the Presidency of Republic of Bulgaria

NATO alley between the Presidency and the Council of Ministers buildings

congruous with market mechanisms. Privatization was delayed by the 'leftist' and 'rightist' governments that used to replace each other; it was turned into an irreversible trend only by the very end of the 20th century. However, in spite of the economic and social problems, Bulgaria gradually adopted the values of democracy. In 2004 the country joined NATO and since January 1, 2007 it became a full member of the European Union.

CONCLUSION

Bulgarian people cares for its ages-old traditions; its music and authentic folklore astound the world with the 'magic of Bulgarian voices'. The intellectual potential of Bulgarians, which has given the world one of the greatest technological discoveries, the computer (it had been invented by the American of Bulgarian origin John Atanasov) remains high. Today Bulgarian scientists work in research institutions all over the world; they also manifest their knowledge and abilities in the field of modern technologies. The entrepreneurial spirit and industriousness, religious and ethnic tolera-

Monument of the maker of the computer John Atanassov, a Bulgarian on his father side, standing in front of Telephone Chamber in Sofia

A group for folk songs with the Public House of Culture in Rodopi town of Zlatograd

The courtyard of Kableshkov's house in the town of Koprivshtitsa. A group of Japanese tourists watch with admiration the performance of Bulgarian folk dance

'St Sofia', symbol of the capital city. A monumental sculpture by the famous Bulgarian artist Georgi Chapkanov

bility, openness towards the world culture, benevolence and traditional hospitability, proved by many generations, are among the highest virtues of Bulgarian nation, both in the past and nowadays.

BULGARIA
AND THE BULGARIANS
A BRIEF HISTORY

Text: Plamen Pavlov, Associate Professor Dr.
Photos: Vyara Kandjeva, Antoniy Handjiyski,
Nikolay Genov,
Photo archive of Bulgarian News Agency
Graphic design: Antoniy Handjiyski
English translation: Vladimir Pomakov
Editor of the Bulgarian text: Vyara Kandjeva
Prepress: Geo Kovatchev

BORINA Publishing House
E-mail: borina@borina.com
www.borina.com